Justin Trudeau

47 Character-Revealing Quotes

from Canada's 23rd Prime Minister

and What They Mean for You

By

Christopher di Armani

Cover Image courtesy of Presidencia de la República Mexicana on Flickr
https://www.flickr.com/photos/presidenciamx/

Published By:

Botanie Valley Productions Inc.
PO Box 507
Lytton, BC V0K 1Z0
http://BotanieValleyProductions.com

Dedication

This book is dedicated to my sweet and loving wife Lynda.
Without her unwavering support none of this would be possible.

Acknowledgements

I would like to acknowledge the many dedicated journalists
who do their jobs with integrity, honour and decency;
who diligently report on the news,
not manufacture it to suit their own personal or political agenda.

I wish there were more of you in mainstream media.

Table of Contents

"Integrity is the lifeblood of democracy.
Deceit is a poison in its veins."

— Edward Kennedy

Foreword

Are you a concerned Canadian citizen?

I am too. That's why the 2015 election bothered me. Not so much because of the man we elected Prime Minister, but because of what the election of that man said about our nation.

Like our American cousins in 2008, Canadians opted for *Hope and Change* in 2015. We opted for style over substance.

ABC – Anything But Conservative became the rallying cry for millions. We rejected serving Prime Minister Stephen Harper as out of touch, distant and without personality. We rejected NDP leader Thomas Mulcair as "Angry Tom." While we, as a nation, were angry at the status quo we did not want an angry man leading our country.

As the American media did with Barack Obama in the lead up to the 2008 US election, our Canadian media completely ignored their anointed candidate's glaring lack of leadership experience and management ability.

That bothered me.

In this book I undertook an examination of Canada's 23rd Prime Minister using Justin Trudeau's own words and actions.

I researched Justin Trudeau's much-publicized missteps and his actions as a result of those missteps. I analyzed the national media's response to the glaring discrepancy between his words and his actions.

My examination uncovered a disturbing pattern. That pattern is the focus of this book.

Are you willing to learn the hard truths about your Prime Minister?

Excellent. Then this book is for you.

Love this book or hate it, I want your honest review on Amazon and Goodreads.

I also want your feedback to me personally.

Use these links to leave your honest review on Amazon and Goodreads, as well as directly to me.

http:// ChristopherDiArmani.net/Review-Trudeau-Book-on-Amazon

http:// ChristopherDiArmani.net/Review-Trudeau-Book-on-Goodreads

http://ChristopherDiArmani.net/Trudeau-Book-Feedback

Sincerely,

Christopher di Armani
Author Extraordinaire
http://ChristopherDiArmani.net

Justin Trudeau's Leadership

"The supreme quality for leadership is unquestionably integrity. Without it, no real success is possible, no matter whether it is on a section gang, a football field, in an army, or in an office."

— **Dwight D. Eisenhower**

Sometimes I Say Stupid Things

"When I get passionate or worked up about an issue, I say things that the Conservatives and opponents and critics like to pounce on."

Are you kidding me?

This book is made possible only by Justin Trudeau's propensity to engage his mouth before his brain. Don't get me wrong. I'm grateful. Were it not for his endless barrage of thoughtless and senseless comments I'd be forced to write about some other politician.

It isn't when he gets passionate or worked up about an issue that causes Justin Trudeau so much trouble. His arrogance, impatience and self-importance do that.

When he speaks from a prepared script Trudeau generally does okay. He *um*'s and *uh's* like a blushing schoolboy caught hiding in the girl's change room only when he's forced off-script.

Despite my dislike for Trudeau the Elder, Pierre excelled at speaking under pressure. He never floundered and he never said stupid things on camera. Well okay, yes, Pierre did say some pretty stupid things but here's the difference.

He never said them without malice of forethought. Trudeau the Elder *always* knew what he said and he meant every word of it.

Trudeau the Younger…. Not so much.

World Stupidity Awards

> *"It is clear that the way forward for Canada will be in a solution that resembles Canada; that is shared values and shared desires for outcomes and different approaches to achieve those outcomes right across this great country."*

Does anyone have a clue what he's babbling about? Does anyone on Planet Earth even understand this sentence?

Didn't think so.

Then consider this.

Justin Trudeau, the man who made that nonsense-filled remark, had the audacity to call the U.S. President dumb.

The World Stupidity Awards are part of the Just For Laughs Comedy Festival. In 2004 Justin Trudeau presented the Stupidity Award for Reckless Endangerment of the Planet to US President George W. Bush.

While Justin Trudeau has yet to endanger the planet, he is well on his way to destroying Canada's middle class.

I think that's worthy of a World Stupidity Award, don't you?

Someone Will Tell Me if Something Important Happens

> *"I don't read the newspapers. I don't watch the news. I figure if something important happens someone will tell me."*

Justin Trudeau made that thoughtful and provocative statement back in 2001. I hope his attitude is a little more substantive today but the evidence points elsewhere.

Oddly, Justin Trudeau made the following candid admission to *MacLean's* reporter Jonathon Gatehouse in December 2002.

"'If enough people put you out there, you become something,' he says, swirling a C.C. and ginger in his hand.

'But I'm far from a finished product. I haven't done anything. I haven't accomplished anything. I'm a moderately engaging, reasonably intelligent 30-year-old, who's had an interesting life-- like someone who was raised by wolves, or the person that cultivated an extremely large pumpkin.'"

Such honesty is rare, even for a person who cultivated an extremely large pumpkin.

Our Childish Prime Minister

"Oh, you piece of sh*t."

Not the language you expect to hear in Parliament, let alone from the man who now holds the highest office in the land. Not even in response to a disingenuous remark from another Parliamentarian, in this case Environment Minister Peter Kent.

NDP Environment critic Megan Leslie asked Minister Kent this question.

"Madam Chair, could the minister give us a rough ballpark of what the budget will be for the delegation? Surely he has a lot of resources at his fingertips, and I am sure that there must at least be an estimate."

Minister Kent responded with a lengthy speech that included this statement.

"Mr. Speaker, if my hon. colleague had been in Durban, she would have seen that Canada was among the leaders in the— As I was saying, Mr. Speaker, if my hon. colleague had not sent a deputy to attend in Durban, she would have seen first-hand how Canada did lead the way in contributing to the creation of the Durban platform. Again, I would remind her and refer her to Nature, which says, 'There is no need to kill [Kyoto]. The treaty is already weakened and will prove hard to revive.'"

At that point Justin Trudeau, disgusted with Minister Kent's response, uttered his rude remark. The day following his outburst Justin Trudeau offered up this half-hearted apology, presumably on orders from his Liberal Party Leader.

> *"I lost my temper and used language that was most decidedly unparliamentary and for that I unreservedly apologize and withdraw my remark."*

It's not the first time Justin Trudeau's childish impatience landed him in hot water, nor will it be the last.

Trudeau's Charity Fundraiser F-Bomb

> *"I will tell you, there is no experience like stepping into this ring and measuring yourself. All the… your name, your fortune, your intelligence, your beauty -- none of that f***ing matters."*

Even when he spoke at a charity event for cancer research Justin Trudeau made it all about his favourite person: Justin Trudeau. Arrogance and ego at the forefront, Trudeau spoke glowingly of his own virtues but he could not do so without injecting profanity.

At Trudeau's post-curse media scrum outside the Ajax-Pickering Board of Trade one reporter asked:

> *"The PMO is saying that your words at the boxing match, specifically the F-word, is an example of your lack of judgment. What do you have to say to that?"*

A smirk on his face, Trudeau offered this rationalization.

> *"Uh… Listen, it was uh fight night at the casino on Saturday night and I found myself once again in a boxing ring and I uh guess I let my emotions uh run a little uh uh a little hot. Uh but rest assured I got an awful lot of uh uh talking to at home from Sophie and uh nothing anyone else can add will be bet… worse than that.*

Uh but it's interesting that someone who would have uh uh had the poor judgment to put Patrick Brazeau or Mike Duffy uh in the senate uh someone who chose uh Arthur Porter, Bruce Carson, or even botched a Supreme Court nomination process uh would be criticizing anyone else uh for judgment."

Humility being Justin's strong point he immediately took responsibility for his actions and sincerely apologized for them.

No? Not quite? Sadly, not even close. Justin Trudeau hid behind Sophie's skirt and then attacked Stephen Harper to deflect the heat from himself.

Why take responsibility for your actions when you can sling mud at your political opponent instead?

When pressed again on the issue of language the man who would become prime minister responded with this:

"Uh... if you had seen the scolding Sophie gave me you would have wished you had used a different adjective as well."

Now that's the sort of leadership Canadians expect, right?

A *London Free Press* online poll asked this question.

"Do you think Justin Trudeau should apologize for swearing?"

A whopping 62% responded with "Yes, it was completely unprofessional."

Even longtime Liberal MP Wayne Easter agreed on that.

"It would have been better not said. However, I think you have to look at, he was doing a charity event, he was doing good work, and I think it was kind of meant to be in a joking style, but as a leader, you can't lay out those kind of jokes."

Our Canadian lapdog media? They dutifully salivated over Trudeau's every word and never once attempted to hold him to account.

Eve Adams a Liberal Candidate? Over My Dead Body!

> *"But most importantly open nominations in our*
> *communities have allowed tens of thousands of*
> *Canadians to participate directly in contested*
> *nominations."*

Conservative MP Eve Adams not only pandered to Justin Trudeau's ego she also took a parting swipe at Prime Minister Stephen Harper while she did it.

> *"I want to work with someone who inspires, not with*
> *fear-mongers and bullies."*

Such sweet words were too much for the Liberal leader to pass up.

Justin Trudeau ignored the fact Adams was already on her way out of the Conservative Party. Her decision to jump ship and take a parting shot at Stephen Harper was motivated by her own sense of political opportunism.

No wonder she appealed to Trudeau.

When longtime Liberal Mike Colle said running former Conservative MP Eve Adams as a Liberal candidate in Eglington-Lawrence would happen "over my dead body" he mistakenly believed Justin Trudeau was sincere about open nominations.

Kelly McParland explained it beautifully in his *National Post* column titled "Who's running the Liberals, Justin Trudeau or Mike Colle's dead body?"

> *"Obviously someone needs to get this message through*
> *to Mr. Colle, before he gets too emotional. He appears*
> *to remain under the impression that local riding*
> *members have a right to run local nominations free*
> *from undue interference from party headquarters, or*
> *from a leader who wants to parachute in favoured*
> *candidates. He may have gotten that impression from*
> *Mr. Trudeau himself, who insisted that was the sort of*
> *party he planned to run. Silly Mr. Colle. Surely he's*
> *been in politics long enough to know that party leaders*
> *often make pledges they don't intend to keep. Did he*
> *think Mr. Trudeau would be different?"*

Trudeau did allow a contested nomination for the riding but he failed to account for one thing: the Liberal Party members of that riding. He assumed his celebrity status would carry the day. He assumed *mere citizens* would do what they're told.

The Liberals Party members of Eglington-Lawrence had other ideas.

They rebuked Justin Trudeau and his ham-fisted attempt to saddle them with a failed political opportunist. They symbolically flipped off their Liberal Party leader and voted for the other guy instead.

This brings into focus a serious question about the man who now sits in Ottawa's big chair.

What was he thinking?

Why is his judgment so out of whack with his own party faithful?

Why is he so eager to collapse back into the same old party politics Canadians universally despise?

Good questions.

Justin Trudeau won't answer any of them.

"How can we reform the Upper House? First, we can tackle the sense of entitlement that a lifetime appointment creates. The Supreme Court has said that senators must have 'security of tenure.' So why not limit the term to 12 years? Today, that's a very 'secure' term in any job."

— Stephen Letwin

Constitution / Legal Rights

Whose Father Created the Charter of Rights and Freedoms?

> *"The segregation of French and English in schools [in New Brunswick] is something to be looked at seriously. It is dividing people and affixing labels to people."*

Justin Trudeau had no clue the Charter of Rights and Freedoms guaranteed Francophones the right to separate schools. Not until the Liberal Party leadership rebuked him for his ignorance, that is.

Michel Doucet is a professor of law at the University of Moncton. Professor Doucet is appalled by Trudeau's constitutional illiteracy.

> *"Mr. Trudeau's statement brought us back by 20 years. I'm surprised to see this from Mr. Trudeau, who is a descendant of the one who signed the Charter and defended this right to linguistic duality."*

An unidentified "senior Liberal source" offered this reprimand.

> *"The Liberal Party of Canada is the party of the Charter that allowed francophones all over the country to obtain their own schools and institutions. What Justin said goes against the Liberal Party of Canada's historical position and shows a flagrant lack of knowledge of the reality faced by francophones who live in minority situations in Canada."*

Even Liberal leader Stéphane Dion found himself backed into a corner by Justin Trudeau's ignorance. Dion did what little he could to distance himself from the Liberal Party's heir apparent.

> *"He is new. He will likely have to explain his thoughts further."*

Explain further he did, tail firmly planted between his legs.

> *"The dualistic nature and the management of*

:hools in New Brunswick are entrenched
ition. It is our Liberal heritage and I am

Acadians and minority francophones, I
ɔ apologize publicly."

Here is Ju.... eau's *modus operandi* in 3 simple steps.

Step 1: Make a stupid statement in public.

Step 2: Be soundly chastised for his ignorance.

Step 3: Offer a half-hearted public apology and pray it all goes away.

This is the Trudeau way. Canada's Media Party dutifully gives Justin Trudeau a pass every time.

Imagine if Stephen Harper or any Conservative MP said "the segregation of French and English in schools… is dividing people and affixing labels to people."

Would the national press be so gentle then?

It's Alberta's Fault and *"we Quebecers, Canada belongs to us."*

> *"Canada isn't doing well right now because it's Albertans who control our community and socio-democratic agenda. It doesn't work,"* Trudeau said in French to interviewer Patrick Lagace.
>
> Lagace asked if Trudeau thought Canada is *"better served when there are more Quebecers in charge than Albertans?"*
>
> *"I'm a Liberal, so of course I think so, yes. Certainly when we look at the great prime ministers of the 20th century, those that really stood the test of time, they were MPs from Quebec… This country – Canada – it belongs to us."*

To blame Alberta for Canada's problems is to express contempt for the economic engine of our nation. To claim "This country - Canada - it belongs to us" is to express contempt for all Canadians.

Yes, Justin Trudeau definitely inherited his father's arrogance.

Alberta MP Jason Kenney described Trudeau's comments on Alberta as typical Liberal arrogance and

> *"the worst kind of divisiveness, the worst kind of arrogance of the Liberal Party, and it brings back for many Westerners the kind of arrogance of the National Energy Program, which of course devastated the Western economy."*

The Liberal Party didn't like Jason Kenney's truthfulness so they did what Liberals do best. They attacked and deflected.

> *"The Conservatives are using out-of-context statements made years ago in a long interview. They are clearly concerned that they are losing the by-election in Calgary Centre and are resorting to smear campaigns to stop their slide. Justin knows that Calgary, Alberta and all of Western Canada are at the very heart of Canada's future.*
>
> *That's a message he has taken to every part of the country, from the beginning of the campaign. We need to get beyond the divisive politics of the Conservatives and include all Canadians."*

Michelle Rempel, another Alberta Conservative MP, called Trudeau's comments ridiculous.

> *"You know, I'm so fired up about this because I am from Alberta and I represent people in the heart of a vibrant, dynamic riding who believe in a strong, national, unified country. And, you know, for Mr. Trudeau to come out and try -- I'm not sure if I heard his statement correctly, it's the first time I heard it -- but for him to try to say,*

'Oh, wait, the Conservatives are smearing me,' rather
than 'I unequivocally apologize for these remarks, they
were wrong, they were ill-informed,' it's ridiculous."

Canadians deserve to know what the future Liberal leader thinks about
Alberta and the rest of Canada. Sun Media reporters researched and
publicized Trudeau's divisive words. There were no political points for
attacking Sun Media so Liberals went after the Conservative Party
instead.

Justin Trudeau says one thing in English Canada and the opposite, in
French, in Quebec. He expresses outrage at English Canada's anger with
his hypocrisy. Justin Trudeau does not realize what he says in Quebec
does not stay in Quebec, not even when spoken in French. He's supposed
to be smarter than that.

"In one fell swoop, this particular interview revives
doubts shared by many in Western Canada about the
federal Liberals," Manon Cornellier said in a blog
post.

"What should they believe? What Justin Trudeau said
only two years ago or what he's saying now, as he seeks
their support in his bid for the Liberal Party of
Canada."

Alberta's economic engine generates billions of dollars in transfer
payments that Alberta sends to *La Belle Provence* every year. Were it
not for Alberta's economy Quebec might well be bankrupt. In light of
that economic reality, Justin Trudeau and the province of Quebec should
express a little gratitude to Alberta, not use it as a national scapegoat.

Federal Support to Quebec

2007/2008	-	$14.62 Billion
2008/2009	-	$15.952 Billion
2009/2010	-	$16,673 Billion
2010/2011	-	$17,267 Billion
2011/2012	-	$17,292 Billion
2012/2013	-	$17,349 Billion

2013/2014	-	$17,907 Billion
2014/2015	-	$19,614 Billion
2015/2016	-	$20,352 Billion
2016/2017	-	$21,402 Billion

Where does Justin Trudeau think those billions will come from after he destroys Alberta's economy? Thin air?

Eventually Justin Trudeau was forced to apologize but that happened only when his own party made it clear there was no other option.

> *"It was wrong to use a shorthand to say Alberta when I was really talking about Mr. Harper's government, and I'm sorry I did that."*

Justin Trudeau's apology lacked so much as a whiff of sincerity.

Justin Trudeau Would Help Quebec Separate

> *"I always say, if there came a point where I thought Canada really was Stephen Harper's Canada, that we were against abortion, against gay marriage, that we went backwards in 10,000 different ways, maybe I'd consider making Quebec a country. Oh yes. Absolutely. I know my values very well, even if I no longer recognized Canada."*

Even when talking about Quebec separation Justin Trudeau must inject abortion into the debate.

Trudeau the Younger would happily drive Quebec's train right out of Canada if we ever passed laws against abortion or same-sex marriage or any of *10,000 different* issues Trudeau promotes.

What an odd position to take given Justin Trudeau's public assertion that his father is his guiding influence.

> *"My father's values and vision of this country obviously form everything I have as values and ideals."*

Justin forgot to add this one little qualifier. Except on Quebec separation.

Young Justin desperately needs a history lesson and nobody is more qualified on the subject than his father. Here, in his own words, is Pierre Elliott Trudeau's thoughts on Quebec separation.

Justin.

Hey.

Justin!

Wake up. Your father is talking to you.

> *"Allow me-perhaps for the last time before going to the polls-allow me to remind you of the essence of the question. There are two issues involved:*
>
> *The first is the sovereignty of Québec, and that is defined in the question itself as: the exclusive power to make its laws, levy its taxes and establish relations abroad; in other words, sovereignty.*
>
> *And while we in this room answer NO, in other rooms in other parts of the province, there are people who answer YES; who truly and honestly want sovereignty.*
>
> *I share your opinion: this is the false option; an option that means, as Jean Chrétien said, that we will no longer send Québec MPs to govern us in Canada; an option that means independence; an option that means the separation of Québec from the rest of the country.*
>
> *To this our answer is NO.*
>
> *But it is not to those who are for or against sovereignty that I wish to address my remarks this evening.*
>
> *After the referendum, I hope we will continue to respect one another's differences; that we will respect the option which has been freely chosen by those who are for or against independence for Québec.*

In this question, therefore, there is sovereignty and there is everything else.

Everything else is a new agreement. It is equality of nations. It is at the same time economic association. It is a common currency. It is change through another referendum. It is a mandate to negotiate. And we know very well what they are doing, these hucksters of the YES vote.

They are trying to appeal to everyone who would say YES to a new agreement. YES to equality of nations. YES at the same time to association. YES at the same time to a common currency. YES to a second referendum. YES to a simple mandate to negotiate.

It is those who say YES through pride of because they do not understand the question, or because they want to increase their bargaining power, and to those among the undecided who are on the brink of voting YES, to whom I am addressing myself this evening, because what we have to ask ourselves is what would happen in the case of a YES vote, as in the case of a NO vote.

And it is the undecided, those who are on the YES side through pride, or because they are tired and fed up, who, in these last few days, must be addressed.

So let us consider this. The Government of Canada and all the provincial governments have made themselves perfectly clear.

If the answer to the referendum question is NO, we have all said that this NO will be interpreted as a mandate to change the Constitution, to renew federalism."

I find it ironic and, yes, oddly pleasing to know the words causing Pierre Elliott Trudeau to roll over in his grave come from the mouth of his own son.

Well done, Justin!

Quebec Deserves More

"We have 24 senators in Quebec and there are only six for Alberta and British Columbia. That benefits us. It is an advantage for Quebec."

This is Justin Trudeau's response to the NDP's policy to abolish the Senate.

Trudeau will not take away Quebec's advantage, no matter the cost to the rest of Canada. The status quo benefits Quebec and Justin is a Quebecer first, foremost and always.

Inside Parliament James Moore took offense. Rightfully so. Moore lashed out at Trudeau and his divisive comments.

"He made it so very clear on this weekend that he doesn't believe in Senate reform 'because we have 24 senators in Quebec and there are only six for Alberta and British Columbia. That benefits us. It's an advantage for Quebec.' All Canadians should be served by national institutions and the Liberal leader should stop dividing Canadians again and again over these matters."

While Trudeau stammered a defense of his Quebec First position in Parliament, Saskatchewan Premier Brad Wall tweeted the following:

"Disappointed in @JustinTrudeau. He opposes abolition because Senate status quo gives advantage to Que over the west."

He isn't the only disappointed provincial leader. Alberta Premier Alison Redford jumped onto Twitter with this:

"Disappointed by @Justin Trudeau's comments. No need to pit AB/BC against regions. We need elected, equal senate, accountable to Cdns."

Not going to happen. An elected, equal senate does not benefit Quebec. Justin Trudeau, as I said, is a Quebecer first, foremost and always. Whenever his divisive statements come back to bite him, Trudeau falls back on the same old, tired defense.

Oops, I made a slip of the tongue. That wasn't what I meant.

It's no shock he repeated that behavior here.

> *"I will admit I am a Quebecer and from time to time when I am speaking with Quebecers I might use the word 'we'."*

Then he let his Quebec superiority escape. He just can't help himself.

> *"The status quo as it is has certain advantages for the East in terms of sheer numerical value and that's not a statement of opinion. That's a statement of fact of what's in the Constitution."*

The ego, the hubris, the sheer arrogance of the man never ceases to amaze.

When Justin Trudeau speaks to Quebecers in French he lets his true feelings out. He behaves like the Prime Minister of Quebec, not the Prime Minister of Canada.

His Quebec First bias lands him in hot water time after time. Well, lukewarm water. The water could only be hot if our mainstream media bothered to pay attention to his pattern.

They don't.

Researching and writing this book taught me Justin Trudeau is a consummate actor. Seldom does his mask crack but when it does Justin's true character seeps out. He can't help it, especially when on his home turf, Quebec.

We *mere citizens* shall rest easy, shan't we, safe in the knowledge our Prime Minister will place Quebec's interests above our own for the next four years.

Justin Trudeau's Hypocrisy on "Open Government"

*"The referendums are pretty good way [sic] of not
getting any electoral reform. Another way of doing is
to make sure that parties that reach out themselves to
fold in a broad diversity of voices and perspectives
within their party, get rewarded as well."*

Prime Minister Justin Trudeau promised a new era of openness and transparency in government.

That idea was so short-lived even I found it hard to believe.

Defend our rights and freedoms from the overreach of Canada's anti-terrorism law? Don't be silly. Electoral reform is far more important.

He wants to change how we elect people to the House of Commons and will do so without consulting Canadians.

Ask yourself who Trudeau's proposed changes will benefit.

Let me give you a hint. It begins with *"Liberal Party of Canada."*

Justin Trudeau favours preferential balloting over our current first past the post system. This will saddle Canada with a Liberal prime minister for the foreseeable future. Being in power 40 of the last 57 years isn't enough for the Liberal Party of Canada. They want more. They want it all.

Cue Justin Trudeau's admiration for China's basic dictatorship.

Our 23rd Prime Minister may be arrogant, self-serving and dictatorial but he's no moron. He understands Liberals benefit most from preferential balloting. Trudeau disagrees with that assessment but he's read the studies.

CBC's Eric Grenier explains.

*"Had a proportional representation system been in
place to decide how the 338 seats in the House of
Commons would be distributed, the Liberals would have
won 134 seats, the Conservatives 109 seats, the New*

Democrats 67 seats, the Bloc Québécois 16 seats and the Greens 12 seats.

With a preferential ballot, voters indicate which candidate is their first choice, second choice, third choice and so on. If no candidate wins a majority of first-choice ballots, the candidate in last place is dropped and those votes are distributed according to who was identified as these voters' second choice.

Candidates continue to be dropped and their votes redistributed until one candidate reaches the 50 per cent threshold, ensuring that a majority of voters get an MP they prefer over at least some of the other candidates."

Eric Grenier worked through the numbers. They prove his theory. Justin Trudeau's choice, preferential balloting, all but guarantees a Liberal majority government.

"Based on this analysis, the Liberals would have seen their seat total balloon from 184 to 224 seats, a gain of 40 seats over their actual performance. The Conservatives' seat total would have slid to 61 from 99, a drop of 38 seats, while the New Democrats would have been boosted slightly to 50 seats from 44. The Greens would not have increased their tally, while the Bloc would have dropped to two seats from 10.

The Liberals benefit from this system because they get almost all of the second-choice support from NDP voters, and are the preferred option for Conservative voters over the New Democrats.

In all, the Liberals would have either placed first or lost on the final ballot in 76 per cent of ridings, compared with 45 per cent for the Conservatives and just 26 per cent for the New Democrats.

That means that Conservative candidates would have been dropped off in a majority of ridings before a winner was decided, while the NDP's candidates would have been dropped off in almost three-quarters of ridings."

The second choice for a New Democrat voter is not Conservative, it's Liberal. Shocking, I know, yet Justin Trudeau insists his choice doesn't benefit the Liberal Party.

> *"Am I in this job to defend a particular political party and ensure that, you know, Liberals get to run this country forever? No. I'm in this job to try and make a significant, positive difference in people's lives."*

Is he so arrogant he believes we *mere citizens* will buy that self-serving and condescending rhetoric?

Yes. Yes, he is.

Of Open Nominations, Winners and... Not Winners?

> *"Any time you have a competitive situation like politics is, there are winners, and there are people who don't win, and their supporters can sometimes be very emotional."*

Barj Dhahan is the man Justin Trudeau spoke of when he issued the quote above. Barj Dhahan didn't "not win" as Trudeau awkwardly claimed. Dhahan was forced out of the nomination race because Trudeau's preferred candidate was Harjit Singh Sajjan.

That would make Barj Dhahan his "not preferred" candidate, I suppose.

Trudeau then explained open nominations don't actually mean *open* nominations.

> *"There were two contestants that were on the path to [being] greenlit. One of them chose to withdraw. Open nominations have never meant anyone who chooses to run can suddenly run. I use the example of Rob Ford. If Rob Ford decided to contest a nomination contest for the Liberal Party, we have a process that says, 'Actually, you're not a Liberal and that crack-smoking thing really doesn't fly with us.' There is a clear process that people have to go through and Barj made a decision to withdraw from the race."*

The not winner was offered another riding, Surrey Centre, and told his candidacy would be acclaimed. That defeated the point for Barj Dhahon. He's lived in the Vancouver South riding for 60 years. Barj Dhahon wanted to represent the riding and the community he knew, not be forced upon another community against their wishes.

> *"They weren't simply offering me to run in [Surrey Centre], they were saying that the nomination would be managed in such a way that I would be the sole candidate -- essentially that I would be acclaimed. I said it's a very interesting proposition, but I decline because Vancouver South has been home to my family for over six decades. ... I have no connectivity, no base in Surrey Centre."*

Rather than be honest about his desire for Sajjan to run unopposed in Vancouver South, Trudeau painted Barj Dhahon as a poor loser instead.

> *"Open nominations, which I continue to be committed to and have always been committed to, is about letting local Liberals choose who is going to be their candidate in the next election."*

Justin Trudeau is committed to open nominations. Local Liberals will choose who represents them in an election.

Unless Justin Trudeau decides to foist his preferred candidate upon them, that is. Then local Liberals must shut up and do as they're told.

I love this new open and transparent Liberal Party of Canada. Such a refreshing change from the Liberal Party of old.

Would-Be Liberal Candidate Christine Innes
Sues Justin Trudeau

> *"Open nominations, which I continue to be committed to and have always been committed to, is about letting local Liberals choose who is going to be their candidate in the next election."*

Justin Trudeau went to great lengths to promote an open and transparent nomination process.

He promised a level playing field for potential Liberal candidates in the 2015 election.

As usual, his actions don't quite measure up.

When your local riding association has no say in the nomination process it is not an open nomination. When your fate rests in the hands of Justin Trudeau's Green Light Committee it is not an open nomination.

Case in point — Justin Trudeau refused to endorse Christine Innes unless she agreed to run in a riding selected for her by Justin Trudeau and his Green Light Committee.

As CBC reported at the time:

> "'This seems to be at variance with the leader's commitment to open and fair nominations. I did make it clear to party leadership, however, that I had an open mind about which riding I would run in in 2015,' Innes wrote in the email.

> 'It was made clear to me that if I did not submit to their demands that they would still get their way. I am now incredibly saddened that those same people have now not only manufactured allegations of apparent intimidation and bullying on young volunteers by my team, but made them public,' she said, referring to unelected backroom advisers."

Justin Trudeau then accused Innes of bullying other potential candidates.

> "'There were no other candidates willing to go near Trinity-Spadina given the approach that this particular team did,' he said following a speech in Kingston, Ont. 'So, we're glad to see there's actually going to be an open nomination now in Trinity-Spadina.'"

Justin Trudeau's definition of open nominations: open to those candidates approved by Justin Trudeau the Liberal Party's Green Light Committee.

> "'Despite the party leadership's public attempts to destroy my reputation I have been encouraged by a number of people from different political stripes to

fight against this unfair and undemocratic action,'
Christine Innes said Monday in reference to taking
legal action."

I found this next tidbit amusing.

Christine Innes offered to drop her defamation lawsuit in exchange for a public apology and donations to the charities Bell Kids Helpline and Equal Voice.

That offer was rejected.

Christine Innes' letter to supporters

I am writing to provide an update to my email to you on Monday.

I am quite shocked to have to tell you that the Liberal Party of Canada has informed me via email this morning that it has decided to not approve my candidacy for the coming by-election in Trinity-Spadina, or for any riding in the 2015 general election.

The party leadership had previously told me they would only approve my candidacy for the by-election in Trinity-Spadina, if I agreed in writing prior to the by-election to run in a pre-assigned riding that would be determined by the Leader of the Party's unelected backroom advisors.

I could not, in good conscience, sign a document-which made no attempt to hide that this new "riding assignment" practice was now the standard practice of the Party. This seems to be at variance with the Leader's commitment to open and fair nominations.

I did make it clear to party leadership, however, that I had an open mind about which riding I would run in in 2015, and would work closely with them after the by-election to ensure the Party's best interests were served. That commitment was not good enough for them which is why they will not approve my candidacy.

It was made clear to me that if I did not submit to their demands that they would "still get their way". I am now incredibly saddened that those same people have now not only manufactured allegations of apparent "intimidation and bullying on young volunteers" by my team, but made them public. These allegations are totally baseless and without merit and were never brought to my attention, as one would have expected in a Party governed by due process.

As someone who has fought long and hard for our Party and our inclusive values, it is not possible for me to reconcile our Leader's repeated commitment to open and fair nominations and to ensuring a "new way of doing politics" with a practice by the party leadership to pre-allocate ridings. I was particularly pleased by our Leader's commitment to openness as my focus within our party has always been on recruiting, mentoring and welcoming new people. The Canadian public's cynicism about politics can only be erased if we as a Party refuse to accept back room deal making and intimidation.

So, it is with much disappointment that I share this news with you. As you know, we had built an enormously passionate and talented team of friends and neighbours. Hundreds of us were ready to hit the streets.

I want to thank all of you who have volunteered with and for me over the years, and taken out memberships to support my candidacy. For me, politics has always been about bringing people together to build stronger communities.

I truly believe that we must use our political system to build a more compassionate society, one that cares for people of all ages and abilities, provides opportunities for newcomers and youth, takes pride in our wealth of culture and diversity, and ensures no one is left behind.

Your friendship and support means the world to me.

Thank you,

Christine Innes

Zach Paikin's Integrity (and Justin's Lack of it)

Zach Paikin may only be twenty-two years old but he comprehends honesty and integrity better than a man twice his age.

Paikin said he believed Justin Trudeau had what it takes to become Canada's next prime minister. Zach Paikin was so enamoured with the Liberal Party leader he put himself forward as a candidate. He announced his run for the Liberal Party nomination in the new riding of Hamilton West-Ancaster-Dundas.

Then Trudeau banned Christine Innes from running in the 2015 election unless she signed off on conditions specifying where she ran, if she was allowed to run at all.

That repulsed young Zach Paikin so thoroughly he canceled his nomination run with this Facebook announcement.

> *"I cannot, in good conscience, campaign to be a part of a team of candidates if others seeking to join that team are prevented from doing so if their ideas or ambitions run contrary to the party leader's interest.*
>
> *I am a strong believer in our country's founding democratic principles, including: Parliament as a place for dialogue, a government that is accountable to Parliament, and party leaders who remain accountable to their respective caucuses. I am particularly troubled by the fact that our leader has discarded some of those principles ultimately in order to protect a star candidate.*
>
> *Blocking nomination bids is what creates the party-wide toxicity we seek to avoid."*

Justin Trudeau believes The Liberal Party of Canada is accountable to him, not the other way around.

Doesn't that just smack of Daddy's arrogance and entitlement?

Rob Ford Need Not Apply

> *"If Rob Ford decided he wanted to run for the Liberal Party in 2015, we'd say, 'No, sorry, the way you approach things, the way you govern, the way you behave is not suitable to the kind of Liberal team we want to build.'"*

Justin Trudeau is absolutely committed to open nominations.

Except when he doesn't like the riding's proposed candidate.

Except when he wants to parachute in his own star candidate.

Your local Liberal constituency association is… free to choose any candidate from Justin Trudeau's approved candidate list.

Real change for the Liberal Party of Canada?

Sounds like the new boss is the same as the old boss.

Just younger. And with better hair.

Referendums are pretty good way of <u>not</u> getting electoral reform

Justin Trudeau wants to change how our nation elects its government. The open and transparent way to achieve that goal is to hold a national referendum.

Let *mere citizens* have their say.

Trudeau is normally a consensus guy yet on electoral reform he is not. National opinion polls confirm Canadians want a referendum on electoral reform. Trudeau ignored our opinions and issued this edict instead.

> *"The referendums are pretty good way of not getting any electoral reform."*

A *Forum Research* poll showed 65 percent of Canadians want a referendum on electoral reform.

"In a random sampling of public opinion taken by the Forum Poll™ among 1429 Canadian voters, as many as two thirds agree a national referendum on electoral reform is required before we change the way MPs are elected (65%).

Fewer than one fifth do not agree a referendum is necessary (18%) and a similar proportion have no opinion (17%).

Agreement a referendum is needed is common to all groups, but especially mid aged groups (45 to 54 - 70%), males (68%), mid income groups ($60K to $80K - 70%), in Atlantic Canada (70%), Alberta (75%), among Conservatives (79%) and New Democrats (75%) but not so much among Liberals (58%) and, curiously, among those who would abolish the monarchy in Canada (70%).

'This is a very conclusive finding. There is a strong majority opinion in favour of a referendum on the way MPs are elected, and it spreads across all regions and socioeconomic groups. It is apparent where public sentiment sits on this complex issue,' said Forum Research President, Dr. Lorne Bozinoff."

Cue Justin Trudeau's personal arrogance and the Liberal Party of Canada's institutionalized arrogance. They know what's best for Canada.

When I want to know Canadians' opinion I will give it to them.

That's the Trudeau way.

That's the Liberal way.

It's NOT the Canadian way.

Trudeau's push to change the way Canadians elect their federal government in understandable. It's best for the Liberal Party.

Unfortunately Justin Trudeau defines what is best for Canadians by what is best for him and his political party. He has no use for the opinions of *mere citizens.*

Fair Vote Canada also condemned Justin Trudeau's self-serving preferential balloting or ranked ballot.

> *"A ranked ballot is not a voting system - it is a feature that can be part of a majoritarian 'winner-take-all' system or of a proportional voting system. Using a ranked ballot in single member ridings, such as those we have today, is a variation of first-past-the-post. It would continue to waste about half of votes cast, produce distorted overall results (false majorities), and replicate many of the problems experienced under our current system. A ranked ballot can also be built into almost any proportional system, such as Single Transferable Vote or Mixed Member Proportional."*

Interim Conservative Party leader Rona Ambrose defended Canadians and their democratic rights against Trudeau's imperialistic diktat.

> *"When you change the rules of democracy, everyone gets to have a say. If the Liberals want to make a fundamental change to our country's voting system, the process must not be dominated by one political party's interests. It is arrogant of the Liberals to believe they are entitled to make a change of this magnitude to our democracy without bringing it directly to the people first. The Conservatives will fight this illegitimate and arrogant Liberal approach every step of the way and demand that all Canadians have a voice through a referendum."*

There are a number of things you can do to diminish this arrogant and self-serving attitude of our employees.

1.   Write Prime Minister Justin Trudeau and demand a referendum on electoral reform. Explain politely why all Canadians must have a say in this fundamental change to our democracy.
http://pm.gc.ca/eng/contactpm

2.   Write Minister of Democratic Institutions Maryam Monsef and do the same. Explain to her a Twitter hashtag is not a national referendum.

3.   Write your personal MP and express politely but firmly any change to the electoral system MUST be done through a national referendum.

4.   Visit http://www.conservative.ca/cpc/protect-your-vote/ and add your name to the list of Canadians who demand a referendum. While this is a partisan list the Conservatives appear to be the ONLY party interested in a referendum on electoral reform. The NDP and Green Party both side with the Liberals.

5.   Listen to Rex Murphy's commentary on electoral reform. It's excellent and will give you many ideas for your letters to our political "betters." http://www.cbc.ca/player/play/689060931669/

6.   Please send me copies of your letters to our elected representatives. My mailing address is below.

> Christopher di Armani
> PO Box 507
> Lytton, BC V0K 1Z0
> email: author@christopherdiarmani.net

I would love to know which arguments you use when talking to our so-called "elected representatives."

Senators Removed from Liberal Caucus

> *"I am the leader of the Liberal Party. I decide who is in the Senate."*

Justin Trudeau's odd move to kick every single Liberal Senator out of the Liberal caucus on January 29, 2014 surprised everyone. Trudeau didn't even inform his Liberal senators until right before his announcement.

> *"As of this morning, only elected Members of the House of Commons will serve as members of the Liberal Caucus. The 32 formerly Liberal Senators are now independent of the national Liberal Caucus. They are no longer part of our parliamentary team.*
>
> *Let me be clear, the only way to be a part of the Liberal caucus is to be put there by the voters of Canada."*

Those former Liberal senators will now sit as independents. They have no official ties to the Liberal Party. So saith Justin Trudeau.

> *"I'm committing today that, if I earn the privilege of serving Canadians as their Prime Minister, I will put in place an open, transparent, non-partisan public process for appointing and confirming Senators. No more closed doors. No more secretive deliberations. No more announcements the week before Christmas, under the cover of darkness."*

What exactly does Trudeau mean with his *open, transparent, non-partisan public process comment*? Does he mean a democratically elected Senate? Maybe. Maybe not.

On one level Trudeau's decision is merely sleight of hand. He wildly waves his right hand and proclaims he did something Brazen and Amazing for All To Witness. With his left he counts the votes to be gained by his trickery.

Pure political smoke screen. Only the most gullible of Canadians believe Liberal senators sitting in their weekly independent caucus meeting are anything other than Liberals.

Am I pessimistic? Absolutely. So was Stephen Harper during Question Period after Trudeau's announcement.

> *"I gather the change announced by the leader today is that unelected Liberal senators will become unelected senators who happen to be Liberal. What the Liberal Party doesn't seem to understand is that Canadians are not looking for a better unelected Senate. Canadians believe, for the Senate to be meaningful in the 21st century, it must be elected."*

Trudeau's sleight of hand gives him political distance from former Senator Harb. The RCMP accused Liberal Senator Mac Harb of fraud. A Senate committee ordered the former Liberal senator to repay over a quarter million dollars.

To the disgraced senator's credit he resigned after he repaid the money.

Conservatives saw Trudeau's self-serving decision for what it was, a way to save himself if the Auditor General's senate report tarnished the Liberal brand.

Justin Trudeau failed to account for how 32 Liberal Senators might respond to his decree they were no longer *Liberal* Senators. They met briefly and came to a decision. They would continue to call themselves Liberals. They would hold regular Senate Liberal Caucus meetings. In other words, they spit on Justin Trudeau's decree.

That possibility never even entered Trudeau's mind.

Then Speaker of the Senate Noel Kinsella agreed to recognize those expelled senators as Liberal. Can you imagine the horror on Justin Trudeau's face?

Yeah, that thought brought a smile to my face, too.

Justin Trudeau's January Senate Announcement

"Canadians want their leaders to be open and straight with them, to tell them the truth. They expect us to come forward with practical solutions that address problems directly.

The Senate has become one of those problems. That, I have heard clearly from Canadians. The Senate is broken, and needs to be fixed.
At the same time, Canadians do not want to re-open the Constitution. They don't want a long, rancorous, and likely pointless debate with the provinces that would distract us from focusing on more important problems.

They want leaders who'll help build an economy that works for all of us, in which everyone has a real and fair chance to succeed. They want us focused on their jobs, their pensions, and a good future for their kids.

So today, I propose an immediate remedy that will not only quell many of the distractions that the current senate is causing, but actually improve its capacity to serve all Canadians.

You see, the Senate is suffering from two central problems: partisanship and patronage.

Let us begin with partisanship.

The Senate was once referred to as a place of sober, second thought. A place that allows for reflective deliberation on legislation, in-depth studies into issues of import to the country, and, to a certain extent, provide a check and balance on the politically-driven House of Commons.

It has become obvious that the party structure within the Senate interferes with these responsibilities.

Instead of being separate from political, or electoral concerns, Senators now must consider not just what's best for their country, or their regions, but what's best for their party.

At best, this renders the Senate redundant. At worst -- and under Mr Harper we have seen it at its worst -- it amplifies the Prime Minister's power.

That is why I have come to believe that the Senate must be non-partisan. Composed merely of thoughtful individuals representing the varied values, perspectives and identities of this great country. Independent from any particular political brand.

And since I believe that real leadership is not just about making campaign promises, I'm taking immediate action, today.

As of this morning, only elected Members of the House of Commons will serve as members of the Liberal Caucus. The 32 formerly Liberal Senators are now independent of the national Liberal Caucus. They are no longer part of our parliamentary team.

Let me be clear, the only way to be a part of the Liberal caucus is to be put there by the voters of Canada.

Further, I challenge the Prime Minister to match this action. As the majority party in the Senate, immediate and comprehensive change is in Conservative hands. I'm calling on the Prime Minister to do the right thing. To join us in making Senators independent of political parties and end partisanship in the Senate.

And by ending partisanship now, we can also end patronage, going forward.

The Senate of Canada is a public institution. It should not be run like the Prime Minister's private club.

Here's what I'm going to do about it. I'm committing today that, if I earn the privilege of serving Canadians as their Prime Minister, I will put in place an open, transparent, non-partisan public process for appointing and confirming Senators.

No more closed doors. No more secretive deliberations. No more announcements the week before Christmas, under the cover of darkness.

We are all poorly served by the way in which Senators are appointed. Canadians especially, yes, but also Members of the House of Commons, even Senators themselves are discredited by the antiquated convention that sees Senators appointed by one person, and one person only.

Eight years ago, Mr Harper railed against this convention as Leader of the Opposition, and committed to change it.
As we know all too well: he didn't. In fact, he embraced this archaic process.

As Prime Minister, he has made 59 appointments, despite his promise to appoint zero. In fact, Mr Harper is the only Prime Minister in our country's 147 year history to appoint the same two people to the Senate twice.

All of these people share one characteristic. The Prime Minister, and the Prime Minister alone, judged them to be useful to himself, and to his party. Mike Duffy, Pam Wallin, Patrick Brazeau, Irving Gerstein are particularly egregious examples of where that leads.

It shows that Mr Harper and the Conservatives have been in power so long that they can no longer tell the difference between their party's interest, and the public interest.

That's poor judgment. More than that, it's just plain wrong.

That is why I call upon the Prime Minister to publicly commit, as I have today, to be guided in all future Senate appointments by an open, transparent, non-partisan process, and once appointed, have senators sit independent from the political parties that serve in the House of Commons.

And in so doing, we will remove partisanship and patronage from the Senate, reforming it and improving it in a deep and meaningful way, without ever having to touch the Constitution of Canada.

Which brings me to my final point.

As an unelected body, there are -- and ought to be -- limits on the Senate's power. These limits have expanded over time and have become conventions. These proposals are in keeping with that direction.

As you all know, the Supreme Court of Canada will rule sometime soon on the exact limits of the House of Commons power as it relates to Senate Reform. Let me be clear on this point: these proposals, while bold and concrete, are not the final word. They represent our judgment of how far we can go in the absence of guidance from the Supreme Court.

In other words, I believe this is the most meaningful action possible without opening up the Constitution. If the Supreme Court says more can be done, we will be open to doing more.
In closing, let me say that there has been a lot of loose rhetoric from the other parties about Senate Reform.

Mr Harper would still have you believe that he is a reformer at heart, despite 8 years of hard evidence to the contrary. Canadians elected his party to bring change to this place. Instead, they got a more virulent version of the status quo: a hyper-political, hyper-partisan Senate that is, more than ever, the Prime Minister's private plaything.

As for Mr Mulcair, his promise to abolish the Senate, as if he had a magic wand, is either deliberately and cynically misleading, or empty and foolish. He knows, or ought to know, that his promise would require the most significant amendment to the Constitution since the creation of the Charter of Rights and Freedoms. Mr Mulcair may want to spend the next decade arguing about the Constitution. I prefer to spend it helping Canadians solve their problems.

At our best, Liberals are relentless reformers. When public institutions fail to serve the public interest, we take bold steps to change them.

We want to build public institutions that Canadians can trust, and that serve Canadians. This requires real, positive change. These proposals are the next step in our Open Parliament plan to do just that.

They won't be the last.

Thank you."

Trudeau's Culture of Entitlement Benefits Politicians

On May 24, 2016 news broke Justin Trudeau would take Wednesday off to spend the day with his equally entitled wife to celebrate their anniversary.

He went to great pains to explain the day would be paid for with personal funds while never answering the actual question put to him, which was:

> *"You're taking a day of downtime tomorrow. Are Canadian taxpayers paying for this downtime in any way, including for idle staffers, and if so, is there any benefit to the country?"*

That's no fawning media softball, is it Justin? No wonder you refused to answer it directly.

Unlike the mainstream media I refuse to sanitize Trudeau's response. What follows are the words of our illustrious Prime Minister in all his stammering glory.

> *"The fact of the matter is we've been working extremely hard... today, uh, and will be at the G7 meetings, uh, on Thursday and Friday, uh, and, uh, in the in the middle of all this, uh, I'm taking a moment to, uh, uh, celebrate on, uh, personal funds, uh, my wedding anniversary with my wife. Uh, this is, uh, the kind of work-life balance that I've often talked about as being essential in order to be able to be, uh, a, uh, ummm, to be in service of the country, uh, with, uh, with, uh, all one's very best and, uh, uh, that's certainly something I'm going to continue to make sure we do."*

While he refused to specify which of the day's expenses will be paid for with personal funds I doubt Trudeau's security detail, meals or hotel are on the list.

As for idle staffers, who knows? Trudeau won't say. I'm sure they'll enjoy the day off with pay while the boss flits about with his wife. On personal funds, of course.

Here at home the list of entitlements just keeps growing. First, he gave Members of Parliament and Senators an 1.8% and 2.1% raise respectively. That doesn't sound like much, right? It's not, I suppose, until you realize two things:

1.   This will cost the *mere citizens* of Canada an additional $1 million per year on top of our federal politicians' already exorbitant wages, and

2.   The raise Trudeau handed himself is four times what he offered federal government workers.

This is where Trudeau's senses of entitlement and hypocrisy collide. Aaron Wudrick of the Canadian Taxpayers Federation put it best.

> *"I don't think most Canadians have much sympathy for the notion that MPs need a pay hike, considering they already earn far more than the average Canadian."*

Far more than the average Canadian is an understatement. The average Canadian earns just over $49,000 per year. The base salary for Members of Parliament is $170,400, 3.5 times that of the average Canadian.

Wudrick totally undersells it with his *far more* comment.

Next is Justin Trudeau's out-of-control spending. On May 19th he announced the $30 billion deficit for fiscal year 2016 was not a hard limit. It could go even higher.

Given Trudeau's penchant for handing over buckets of Canadian taxpayer cash to foreign nations that amount will likely be much higher.

He dished out those buckets of cash to foreign governments while he maintained complete radio silence on the Fort McMurray wildfire disaster.

He couldn't remain silent on Fort McMurray forever though. When he finally rediscovered his voice Justin Trudeau said he would "match Red Cross donations."

Every Canadian ought to view this as a slap in the face. Here's why.

Sun Media's Ottawa correspondent David Akin researched Trudeau's spending binge outside the country in the first 100 days of his reign.

The result is a mind-numbing $5.3 billion.

Yes, that's with a "B".

In that same 100 days he spent less than $1 billion *inside* Canada's borders.

The best he can do for Fort McMurray is match Red Cross donations?

That's insulting.

Justin Trudeau's priority is to dole out billions of Canadian taxpayer cash overseas. Let's not forget those numerous and all-important selfies.

The *mere citizens* of Fort McMurray? They don't make the cut.

When even the *Huffington Post* calls out Trudeau for sending too much cash out of the country (Trudeau's Spending Priorities Send Too Many Tax Dollars Overseas) things must really be bad. Unfortunately for Canadians the news only gets worse.

The National Bank projects Trudeau's Liberal government will pile an additional $90 Billion onto Canada's already massive national debt by the next federal election. That's on top of the $30 billion he added in Year One.

Mere Citizens!

Hang onto your wallets.... and hang on tight. Emperor Trudeau is coming for them and he won't take "No" for an answer.

Taxpayer-Funded Nannies

> *"In these times, Mr. Harper's top priority is to give wealthy families like his and mine $2,000. Let me tell you something: We don't need it. And Canada can't afford it."*

His rhetoric to the contrary, Justin Trudeau's Entitlement Syndrome kicked into high gear the moment he won the election. He proclaimed *we don't need it* during the election campaign but what was Trudeau's very first order of business as Prime Minister?

He hired two nannies at taxpayer expense. You cannot expect wealthy families like Justin Trudeau's to pay for their own child care. Absolutely not. The very thought is outrageous!

Outrageous is exactly what Canadians thought when they learned of Trudeau's face-plant into the taxpayer trough.

A poll commissioned by *TheRebel.Media* showed 70% of Canadians believe Justin Trudeau should pay for his nannies with his own money. Perhaps from, say, his multi-million dollar trust fund?

Only in British Columbia and Ontario did that number drop below 70%; 62% in British Columbia and 67% in Ontario.

Jason Kenney rightfully jumped on Trudeau for his sense of entitlement.

> *"Nannies not separate. [sic] Harpers paid for babysitters, not taxpayers and they didn't inherit millions. Nor did Laureen whine about it."*

But I think Ezra Levant said it best on Sept. 26, 2016 when he tweeted the following message:

> *"When your boss hires two nannies on the taxpayer dime the staff figure out the political culture pretty quickly."*

Justin Trudeau knows entitlement. He was raised on it. Prior to entering politics Justin Trudeau did as he pleased, safe in the knowledge his every whim was backed by his father's trust fund.

Seriously, who can blame Trudeau the Younger's belief he is entitled to taxpayer-funded nannies? It's a page from *The Entitlement Handbook* penned by his father. Pierre Elliott Trudeau also forced taxpayers to pay the freight for his family's child care.

The apple of entitlement sure doesn't fall far from the tree.

On a slightly different note, the CBC reports Justin Trudeau is eligible to receive $3,400 in child support payments annually for his three children. Also according to the CBC, Justin Trudeau promised he would give that money to charity.

I would love to know which charity received Mr. Trudeau's child care benefit. And whether he demanded a tax receipt for his generous donation. Given his ongoing hypocrisy it is more likely he forgot that promise the moment he signed papers ordering the *mere citizens* of Canada to pay for his nannies.

I Have Tremendous Confidence...

"I have tremendous level of confidence in ordinary people who go through their lives, don't think a lot about politics, don't think a lot about terrorism..."

What an astonishing expression of desire for dictatorial powers.

"Wait just a minute there, di Armani," you say. *"He said he has a 'tremendous level of confidence' in people who don't pay attention to politics or terrorism. How can you possibly twist that to mean Justin has an astonishing desire for dictatorial powers?"*

With shocking ease, truth be told. Allow me to ask you a simple question. Two, actually, then I'll explain.

Who does the political leader of any nation despise? Who, without fail, will bring about that political leader's early demise?

An informed citizen engaged in the political process.

Politicians at every level of government despise informed and engaged citizens, and for the same reason. Informed and engaged citizens hold politicians to account. Politicians hate accountability.

Trudeau wants no part of an informed and politically active citizenry. He admires the opposite: an *uninformed* citizenry *disconnected* from the political process.

When you get right down to it, isn't that the warm wet dream of every politician?

Our Prime Minister "has a tremendous level of confidence in" *mere citizens* who will follow him blindly and without question.

Aren't you the least bit curious why?

"We don't have a trillion-dollar debt because we haven't taxed enough; we have a trillion-dollar debt because we spend too much."

— Ronald Reagan

Economics / Fiscal Policy

Are You Part of Justin Trudeau's Middle Class?

On three separate days *Ottawa Sun* reporter David Akin pressed Justin Trudeau for a definition of what income level constituted the middle class.

> *"You want a figure?" he replied. Yes, please!*
>
> *He didn't have a figure. Instead he said:*
>
> *"There are all sorts of different ways of calculating which decile or quintile constitutes the middle class. The reality is that I consider the middle class is people who work for their income, not people who live off their assets and their savings."*

If you work for a living you are in the middle class and if you're retired you are not. Pretty simple, except for one thing, as Akin pointed out.

> *Huh? People who "live off their assets and their savings" are pretty much every retired person in this country. Sorry, grandma, you're out of Trudeau's middle class but Gord Nixon, who was paid $12.7 million last year as the CEO of the Royal Bank, you and your bank CEO buddies "who work for their income" are in the middle class!*

Akin went back to Trudeau with a hope for a remotely sensible answer. He received this answer instead.

> *"I have been very clear that people who live off their incomes are of the middle class and those who live off their assets, their portfolios, their trust funds are not."*

He is absolutely positively clear that Royal Bank CEO Gord Nixon, who lives off his income of $12.7 million per year is middle class.

Grandpa, with his annual pension of $30,000 is not.

Great. Got it. Thanks Justin.

David Akin wasn't finished but before he could tell Justin why he was confused Trudeau defined his position once and for all.

> *"For me, it's people who live paycheck to paycheck,"* he said.

Hang on a minute.

On Tuesday Justin Trudeau was "very clear" about Monday's answer which was, by Wednesday, different again.

The only consistent part of Trudeau's ever-changing definition of middle class is this: retired people are not included in the middle class.

Precisely who *does* Justin Trudeau consider middle class?

I have no idea. Canadians living paycheck to paycheck probably consider themselves working poor. Anyone earning a million dollars a month probably considers themselves wealthy.

Not our Prime Minister.

We Need the Middle Class To Feel More Confident

> *"We need the middle class to feel more confident about its prospects and about its future. We need to cut down on this anxiety that sees some people succeeding and the majority struggling - having to make choices between paying for their kids' education or saving for their own retirement."*

Justin Trudeau made that statement in a long and rambling interview with the *Ottawa Citizen*. This interview took place before he won the 2015 federal election.

His entire statement is below, followed by my examination of it.

> *"When I get out across the country and listen to people, the resentment that I see and the frustration that I see is that we have a generation of people who are fairly convinced that their kids are not going to have a better quality of life or a better future than they will.*
>
> *The fact that over the past generation, median household income has stalled, increased by only 15 per cent when our GDP has more than doubled in size.*
>
> *It means that something isn't working any more. And it goes to more than just an idea of redistribution. I regularly talk about this. I talked about this on Bay Street when I gave a speech a few months ago. I talk about this in fundraisers to very wealthy Canadians where I say, 'Look, the problem is not one of redistribution as much as it is a problem of growth.'*
>
> *We need the middle class to feel more confident about its prospects and about its future. We need to cut down on this anxiety that sees some people succeeding and the majority struggling – having to make choices between paying for their kids' education or saving for their own retirement.*
>
> *And making sure the middle class has a little more money in their pockets to invest, to save, to grow the economy is good for everyone."*

There are many problems with Trudeau's thoughts on the middle class. Let's start with his take on median household income and GDP.

> *"The fact that over the past generation, median household income has stalled, increased by only 15 per cent when our GDP has more than doubled in size. It means that something isn't working any more. And it goes to more than just an idea of redistribution."*

The 15% increase Trudeau complained about is not a Canadian phenomenon, it's a North American one. Since 1980 the US GDP increased 67% while the median US household income increased by only 15%.

This is not news. If any party is to blame it would be the Liberal Party of Canada since they formed government 40 of those years since 1963. A Conservative party was in power just 17 years: eight under Brian Mulroney and nine under Stephen Harper.

Joe Clark's six month stint as Prime Minister between two Pierre Elliott Trudeau administrations doesn't count.

Justin Trudeau complains *something isn't working any more. And it goes to more than just an idea of redistribution.*

Canada's national debt rose from $14.8 billion in 1962 to $612.3 billion in 2015. Pierre Elliott Trudeau skyrocketed Canada's national debt from $18.75 billion to $157 billion during his tenure as Prime Minister.

Justin Trudeau is happy to follow Daddy's example. He added $30 billion to our national debt in 2016, with another $113 billion promised by the end of his term.

It's easy to see what's not working, but only if you open your eyes. *Government* is what's not working. Government cannot continue to spend money like a drunken sailor and expect there will be no consequences for our nation.

Trudeau offers no solutions. He just wants us to *feel better*.

> *"We need the middle class to feel more confident about its prospects and about its future. We need to cut down on this anxiety that sees some people succeeding and the majority struggling..."*

With Canada's version of Hope and Change in the Prime Minister's office this will not end well for the *mere citizens* of Canada.

It's hard "to feel more confident about our prospects and about our future" with our Prime Minister face-down in the taxpayer trough.

The US national debt reached a staggering $10 trillion when George Bush left office. Barack Obama's greatest accomplishment in 8 short years? He doubled the US national debt. It will be $19.5 trillion by the time he exits the Oval Office.

That dereliction of duty by American President Barack Obama is Justin Trudeau's roadmap for Canada, despite how he ends his diatribe:

> *"And making sure the middle class has a little more money in their pockets to invest, to save, to grow the economy is good for everyone."*

We would love to keep more of what we earn. That's not possible when our Prime Minister delivers carbon taxes, a mountain of debt and God knows what else between now and 2019.

Justin, it's simple. If you want Canadians to have more money in their pockets stop your feel-good taxation and lose your spending addiction.

Promise Kept or Promise Broken?

> *"We will save home mail delivery. By ending door-to-door mail delivery, Stephen Harper is asking Canadians to pay more for less service. That is unacceptable. We will stop Stephen Harper's plan to end door-to-door mail delivery in Canada and undertake a new review of Canada Post to make sure that it provides high-quality service at a reasonable price to Canadians, no matter where they live."*
> — Liberal Party website

The Liberal Party website says a Trudeau government will *stop Stephen Harper's plan to end door-to-door mail delivery in Canada.* Then it launches into obfuscation mode.

Trudeau's government will *undertake a new review of Canada Post to make sure that it provides high-quality service at a reasonable price to Canadians, no matter where they live.*

At no time does Trudeau or the Liberal Party say they will *restore* home delivery to thousands of Canadians. They commit to, at best, *"a new review of Canada Post to make sure that it provides high-quality service at a reasonable price to Canadians, no matter where they live."*

Allow me to translate.

The Trudeau government will meet about it, talk about it and "study the issue" until so much time passes that Canadians resign themselves to defeat.

Less service from Canada Post is the new normal.

It's Trudeaupian double-speak worthy of George Orwell's *1984*.

Public Services Minister Judy Foote, strangely enough, managed some rare Liberal honesty.

> *"There's a potential here for restoring home mail delivery. The question is, is it restored on a two-day a week, three-day a week, five-day a week -- we need to hear from Canadians what they need. So it could be anything from a shorter period of time to a longer period of time."*

Wait a minute. Restoring home delivery is now *a potential*?

That's not what the Liberal Party promised Canadians during the campaign.

The Canada Post review committee released its interim report in September 2016. It highlighted Canada Post's financial plight — massive pension commitments and continuing revenue decline.

I found their conclusion about Canada Post's community mailbox conversion far more interesting.

> *"When Canada Post put forward its plan in 2013 to convert approximately 5 million addresses (32% of the total 15.8 million addresses served by Canada Post) from door-to-door delivery to community mailboxes, savings were projected to be identified as being between $400 and $500 million annually.*

This estimate has since been revised to $400 to $450 million, based on lessons learned from the first wave of implementation. That first wave included 830,000 addresses and is projected to generate $80 million per year in savings.

To better contextualize the complexity of the conversion to the community mailbox program, it is worthwhile to note that Canada Post had to invest a net amount of over $240 million to implement these conversions.

This level of investment illustrates that Canada Post needs considerable financial resources to reduce ongoing costs, which will not be easy to achieve. The main reasons for the reduced long-term savings are as follows:

- *lower efficiencies than anticipated*
- *longer implementation process than planned*
- *Introduction of an accommodation program for those with mobility issues*

The degree of resistance in major cities with the proposed conversion strategy was not initially anticipated by Canada Post and the corporation was forced to adjust its plans in response to local concerns, which led to the revised savings target.

This revised target of $400 to $450 million has been assessed by Ernst & Young to be reasonable. Estimated annualized savings have been found to be sound, robust and based on defensible assumptions."

Do you honestly believe Justin Trudeau will reinstate Canada Post home delivery after reading that?

When will Canadians learn that from this age-old political maxim?

How do you know a politician is lying?

Their lips are moving.

Small Businesses are Frauds and Tax Evaders

> *"We have to know that a large percentage of small
> businesses are actually just ways for wealthier
> Canadians to save on their taxes and we want to reward
> the people who are actually creating jobs and
> contributing in concrete ways."*

Dan Kelly, president of the Canadian Federation of Independent Business, took great offense at Trudeau's characterization of small business owners.

> *"As the largest small business group in Canada, we
> see no evidence that the small business rate is being
> used by so-called wealthier Canadians to save on their
> taxes."*

Research by Kelly's organization shows almost half of incorporated Canadian employers, in other words small businesses, earned less than $50,000 last year. The overwhelming majority, 80%, earned less than $100,000 last year.

Wealthier Canadians saving on their taxes?

Hardly.

Justin Trudeau's characterization of Canada's small business owners as frauds and tax cheats is thoughtless and without merit.

> *"One of the things I have been consistent in
> throughout my tenure as leader is an approach that
> actually doesn't worry too much about how my
> opponents might choose to attack me on a given
> statement,"* Trudeau said.

That's sound policy for a man who routinely delivers such thoughtless rhetoric. My personal preference is for Justin Trudeau to support Canadian small business owners. You know, the folks who actually create jobs.

What's that? It's *government* that creates jobs?

I don't think so, Justin.

According to the Innovation, Science and Economic Development Canada website (Yes Justin, your government's website) small businesses accounted for 70% of all jobs in 2016, down slightly from 77% in 2013. Supporting job creators is a proper role for government.

Calling those job creators lying tax evaders… not so much.

Government's Shouldn't Go Into Debt

"I believe in fiscal responsibility and I quite frankly, I think Liberals who believe that the government should be doing things well and should be doing some certain things are more motivated to therefore to do them well, do them responsibly, not going to massive deficits the way certain other governments who have been less motivated to deliver good government have."

That statement, delivered by Justin Trudeau on CNN's foreign affairs show *Fareed Zakaria GPS*, is truly bizarre. Justin Trudeau campaigned on running a $10 billion deficit.

Unfortunately for Canadians, Trudeau kept his word on that promise, and more.

When voted out of office Conservatives left Justin Trudeau's Liberals a gift in the form of a $1.9 billion surplus. He was barely sworn in before he burned through that surplus, galloping to a $34 billion deficit for fiscal 2016/2017 alone.

Trudeau promised Canadians deficits would reach $30 billion in the first three years of his term. He accomplished that dubious goal in his first year.

Not exactly the Sunny Ways Justin Trudeau promised Canadians.

He will add more than $113 billion to the federal debt in just four short years but that's not even the worst news.

The Trudeau government has no plan to return to a balanced budget.

None.

His actions are in direct opposition to his stated beliefs.

By his own words that identifies Justin Trudeau's government as one *less motivated to deliver good government.*

During his budget speech to the House of Commons, Finance Minister Bill Morneau trumpeted that age-old mantra guaranteed to silence all opposition across political lines, regardless of subject: "It's for the children."

> *"We act for the years and decades to come. We act for our children and our children's children."*

Really?

Bill Morneau and Justin Trudeau must really despise their children, their children's children and even their children's children's children.

How else do you explain their willingness to bury a generation not yet born under a mountain of debt and offer no plan to dig them out?

Deficits measure growth and government success

> *"Deficits are a way of measuring the kind of growth and the kind of success that a government is actually able to create."*

Justin Trudeau is correct. Deficits are a measuring stick for governments. He falls off the rails with his conclusion that deficits measure government success. They do not. They measure that government's failure.

The $34 billion deficit he saddled us with in Year One measures Justin Trudeau's personal failure. His father's failure, too, for this is the economic lesson he taught his son.

Every single taxpayer is on the hook for the irrational and wasteful spending of governments at all levels, be it municipal, provincial or federal.

A nation, just like the *mere citizens* who comprise that nation, must live within its means. Justin Trudeau, like his father before him, ignores that reality.

When you spend more money than you possess (or take from *mere citizens*) you must borrow the difference. The lender charges for that pleasure by levying a fee we call *interest*. Debt and the interest charged on debt is a burden on ordinary Canadians and our entire economy. Justin Trudeau's contention that the *commitment needs to be a commitment to grow the economy* and the budget will balance itself is sheer economic lunacy.

Yes, a stronger economy means more revenue for government which *ought* to mean lower deficits. It *ought* to mean paying down the nation's debt too. Somehow that never happens though, does it?

Under Justin Trudeau the federal government is committed to a carbon tax, a scheme even the United Nations admits is rife with corruption worldwide.

Under Justin Trudeau the federal government is committed to putting the Alberta Oil Sands out of business.

He favours importing oil from such bastions of personal freedom as Saudi Arabia instead of developing Canada's natural resources to make our nation energy self-sufficient.

Why should Trudeau care?

He's never faced such trivialities as earning a living or penny-pinching to make ends meet. Such trivialities are the domain of those *mere citizens* forced to pay for Trudeau's excesses.

His words are, as always, at odds with his actions. Trudeau promises one thing yet does another. He wants to help the middle class but imposes a carbon tax that directly harms them.

He wants more money in middle class wallets, yet dumps billions of tax dollars into other nations, money he must borrow first and we *mere citizens* must pay back. Our grandchildren, actually, if we're honest with ourselves.

Yes, Justin.

Deficits measure government success and the budget will balance itself.

Growing the Economy from the Heart Outwards

> *"We're proposing a strong and real plan, one that invests in the middle class so that we can grow the economy not from the top down the way Mr. Harper wants to, but from the heart outwards."*

What?

The *National Post* headline said it best:

> *"Justin Trudeau promises to grow the economy 'from the heart outwards' -- whatever that means"*

The *Toronto Sun* mocked *Trudeau's Care Bear Economics* in their editorial.

Trudeau attempted to clarify his statement with this Twitter post.

> *"Great to talk to people in Regina about our plan to strengthen the heart of the Canadian economy: the middle class."*

Justin Trudeau defecated all over small business owners by calling them tax evaders. Is this his idea of strengthening the economy and investing in Canada's middle class?

> *"We have to know that a large percentage of small businesses are actually just ways for wealthier Canadians to save on their taxes and we want to reward the people who are actually creating jobs and contributing in concrete ways."*

Racking up back-to-back $30+ billion deficits is *investing in the middle class*? I do not understand. Then again I'm nothing but one of Trudeau's cash cows, er, I mean *mere citizens*.

Taxpayers. I meant to say *taxpayers*.

I'm nowhere near as smart as Justin Trudeau claims to be.

I accept that.

Spending money we don't have is a *good* thing. How silly of me. Where I come from that's called living beyond our means. It is a recipe for disaster but, as I said, I'm nowhere near as smart as Justin Trudeau claims to be.

Prime Minister Pierre Elliott Trudeau increased Canada's national debt by 787%. He almost bankrupted Canada when he racked up a debt so massive it took Canadians a generation to recover.

Yes, Justin Trudeau knows how to grow an economy. He learned about it at the feet of his father, who spent money we did not have like a drunken sailor.

Now we're going to do it again.

Say it with me….

> *"Justin Trudeau saddled Canadians with a thirty-four billion dollar deficit in his very first year in office. He promised to do the same thing in his second year. And his third. And his fourth."*

Do you feel all sick inside now?

Me too.

We Must Price Carbon!

> *"I think we need to price carbon; there's no question about it. The way we do it needs to be based on science and not political debates and attacks, and that's why I'm drawing on experts and best practices from around the world."*

There is nothing a Limousine Liberal loves more than a tax, especially one that embraces collective western guilt.

Justin Trudeau proudly announced his carbon tax pandering to that guilt. In doing so, Trudeau also revealed he does not comprehend Canada's economic reality.

Canada faces three problems with Trudeau's carbon tax.

First, our entire economy runs on oil and gas. It heats our homes and businesses. It powers our vehicles and the transport trucks that move goods to market across the nation. A carbon tax immediately increases the cost of living for Canadian families. A carbon tax guarantees our products and services are less competitive outside our borders.

Second, there is no such thing as a carbon price.

It's a fallacy, a wealth redistribution scheme dreamed up by politicians and environmental extremists.

Third, carbon tax schemes are corrupt in every single jurisdiction worldwide, without exception. That's not some crazy conservative speaking either. That's straight from the United Nations.

Lorne Gunter of the Edmonton Sun explains further:

> "[N]o market exists for carbon emissions except where governments force companies to buy or sell 'carbon credits.' Therefore, there is no such thing as a natural 'carbon price.' The concept is entirely artificial.

> "Admittedly, Europe has a carbon exchange, but it's not a real marketplace like a stock exchange. It wouldn't exist if the EU's commissioners hadn't dictated that companies put a price on their emissions and pay extra for emissions above their mandated limits. Even after all of that, the price for a tonne of carbon on the European exchange is a fraction of what EU planners projected it would be.
> The only people who make money consistently are clever profiteers who have learned how to apply for 'green' subsidies. And the whole thing is prone to corruption."

David Suzuki describes it this way:

> "A carbon tax is a fee placed on greenhouse gas pollution mainly from burning fossil fuels. This can be done by placing a surcharge on carbon-based fuels and other sources of pollution such as industrial processes."

Isn't that the epitome of Sweetness and Light and All Things Good?

Now read the last half of Suzuki's final sentence once more.

"and other sources of pollution such as industrial processes."

That's *Suzuki-speak* for Alberta's oil sands. Environmental extremists and Limousine Liberals call them Alberta's tar sands. Extracting petroleum from Alberta's oil sands is, in the eyes of these extremists, evil and nasty and to blame for All The World's Problems.

Punish Alberta's oil sands. Tax them out of existence, they cry.

Trudeau's hypocrisy on the carbon tax is palpable. He champions the middle class. His carbon tax will steal another $2,500 from the wallets of every single Canadian family every year. If that's your idea of supporting middle class families, Mr. Trudeau, I want no part of it.

Then there is the issue of corruption that permeates every carbon tax scheme known to man.

> *"The implementation of cap-and-trade systems in both developed and developing countries has been recurrently tainted by cases of fraud and bribery, abuses of power, and other conventional forms of corruption.*
>
> *Corruption in this sector has also taken more original forms, such as the strategic exploitation of 'bad science' and scientific uncertainties for profit, the manipulation of GHG market prices, and anti-systemic speculation (Lohmann, 2007; TI, 2012a; Wara, 2007).*
>
> *The challenge that corruption poses to climate finance also contributes to broader debates about the impact of corruption in environmental governance.*
>
> *Over the past two decades, domestic and international anti-corruption initiatives have proliferated, with the process being largely driven by the increasing recognition of the impact of corruption on the quality of environmental governance.*
> *For the first time, the participants in the 2012 United Nations Conference on Sustainable Development (or the Rio+20 Conference) explicitly recognised that*

corruption is an impediment to effective environmental stewardship: paragraph 266 of the Outcome Declaration – The Future We Want – proclaimed that corruption must be addressed for the successful allocation and effectiveness of international aid.

In the document, governments stressed the links between transparency and accountability and the quality of governance, noting that 'corruption is a serious barrier to effective resource mobilisation and allocation and diverts resources away from activities that are vital for poverty eradication, the fight against hunger and sustainable development' (UN, 2012, pp.50).

They also recognised the need to 'take urgent and decisive steps to continue to combat corruption in all its manifestations' (UN, 2012, pp.50). This attention to the issue of corruption in the Rio+20 Declaration echoes the debates that have taken place during the past decade in conferences and policy initiatives organised and implemented by the United Nations Office on Drugs and Crime (UNODC), the European Union, the Association of Southeast Asian Nations (ASEAN), the G20, and other multilateral organisations.

In the face of challenges some critics have begun questioning the validity of the fundamental tenets of emissions trading schemes, but supporters of the approach have responded by beginning to mainstream anti-corruption strategies into their frameworks and paying more attention to the consequences of corruption on the overall efficiency of the system."

When it is so widespread, so rampant and so systemic even the United Nations cannot hide from the truth, carbon tax corruption must truly be horrendous.

Then there is that pesky little fact Justin Trudeau will not face. Canada's entire greenhouse gas emissions account for less than two per cent of all global emissions.

Canada is not the problem.

Tanking our economy and impoverishing our middle class will not solve the problem either.

Trudeau's much-admired Chinese dictatorship is the world's largest greenhouse gas emitter. China's CO_2 output more than doubles that of the second-place United States. China emits almost one third of all greenhouse gas emissions in the world. They are building coal-fired power generation plants at the rate of two new facilities per week.

China has no carbon tax.

Justin Trudeau will never admit his carbon tax is economic suicide for Canada. He will never admit it is a direct attack on Canada's middle class, either.

He's too busy basking in the glorious rays of adoration from his environmental acolytes at the United Nations.

"I cannot believe that while the country's environment ministers were meeting on a so-called collaborative climate change plan, the prime minister stood in the House of Commons and announced a carbon tax unilaterally. This meeting is not worth the CO_2 emissions it took for environment ministers to get there. The level of disrespect shown by the prime minister and his government today is stunning."

— Saskatchewan Premier Brad Wall

Social Issues / Human Rights

Welcomed, Not Feared

"We want these families arriving to be welcomed, not feared, because that's the way to get the right start in terms of having them become valuable parts of our community and create success."

Justin Trudeau backed off his year-end deadline to bring 25,000 Syrian refugees into Canada. This is one promise I'm happy to see broken.

Hopefully the Liberal government will now screen refugees properly before they hit our shores. Canadian law is clear. Once refugees land on Canadian soil they cannot be removed.

While I have no problem bringing people from war-torn nations to Canada the federal government's mandate is to protect Canadians here at home, first. Our federal government must take that mandate seriously if Justin Trudeau expects *mere citizens* to embrace his refugee plan.

Here's the trouble. Placing twenty-something Syrian men who do not speak English into Canadian high schools is causing problems. Big problems. Trouble at a single school in New Brunswick reveals how horribly Trudeau's refugee plan is backfiring.

"Last week an article by the Chronicle Herald detailed multiple instances of Syrian refugees assaulting Canadian children. The article featured comments by a woman nicknamed 'Missy' who explained how her daughter had been choked with a chain and her son had been visibly threatened on the soccer field.

The story was pulled soon after it was posted with members of the left-wing media decrying the story as 'racist,' 'Islamophobic,' 'xenophobic' or simply just not true.

In place of the story, an apologetic message was left in its place saying the story needed more research and was 'insensitive' to the refugees."

TheRebel.Media reporter Faith Goldy dug into the story after *Chronicle Herald* reporters would not. She discovered some interesting facts. She met with the mother of the young girl choked by Syrian boys at school. "Missy" confirmed the following:

> *"They need help in the school. They need*
> *communicators. Interpreters. Teachers. And more than*
> *one, Monday to Friday. They can't have an interpreter*
> *up there two days a week. There's kids that speak*
> *Arabic five days a week."*

> *"They said in the paper she was choked with chains*
> *two different times. That wasn't what was said. She*
> *was choked twice, but once with a necklace. She was*
> *choked with their hands. Like it was just a bunch of*
> *little stories that kept adding up and I was like this is*
> *enough. Like, once or twice it happens, maybe it's just*
> *rough play. But it's happening a lot. And it hasn't just*
> *been this week. There has been numerous things that*
> *have happened. Not just with my kids."*

> *"We went up on Friday to talk to the principal about the*
> *choking with the necklace, she said that her hands are*
> *tied. She said that she's been fighting with her supervisor*
> *to get interpreters up there because she couldn't contact*
> *those kids' parents. And was here Friday. It's been a*
> *whole week that that wasn't addressed."*

> *"Yesterday my daughter was slapped in the face again*
> *by the exact same boy. Again. We got called up to the*
> *school and they had an interpreter in there yesterday*
> *and she said, the interpreter said, the little boy just wants*
> *to fit in."*

Nobody would believe *TheRebel.Media*, of course. It's a nasty right-wing news organization who employs a nasty right-wing Roman Catholic reporter.

I jest, of course. I've met Faith Goldy. She's delightful. She lives her Roman Catholic faith and she is tenacious when confronted by injustice.

I thank God for that.

Everything Faith Goldy wrote is a result of her questions to Fredericton parents and from culling through over 2,700 pages received through Access to Information Requests.

Global News reluctantly admitted Goldy did not make it up; that the documents were, in fact, from Fredericton High School. I'm sure that endorsement almost killed them but what choice did they have?

Chantal Lafargue, department head for international students at Fredericton High School, confirmed the validity of the documents in a March 30, 2016 email.

> *"We are living in a province where there are no official EAL (English as an alternative language) courses for high school, no alternate programming for war-affected youth, no personnel that have designated roles, like translator-interpreters, for example to help us settle youth down, make them feel at ease and help them navigate a whole new set of cultural and social norms."*

Bringing refugees to our shores from war-torn nations is a good thing, but we must ensure resources are in place *before* those refugees arrive.

Justin Trudeau?

His Syrian refugee photo op, along with the requisite number of selfies, was a rousing success. That was the end of it. Until another selfie opportunity presents itself, of course.

Ensuring our communities have the resources to deal with the massive influx of refugees? That's not Trudeau's problem.

No, that problem rests on the shoulders of young girls and boys in schools like Fredericton High. They must pay the price for Justin Trudeau's photo ops and, let us not forget, his all-important selfies.

Justin Trudeau is offended by the word "barbaric"

> *"There's nothing that the word 'barbaric' achieves that the words 'absolutely unacceptable' would not have achieved."*

Celebrity feminist and Liberal Immigration Critic Justin Trudeau delivered that condemnation in response to the updated wording of an Immigration Canada pamphlet.

> *"Canada's openness and generosity do not extend to barbaric cultural practices that tolerate spousal abuse, 'honour killings,' female genital mutilation, forced marriage or other gender-based violence."*

Spousal abuse, 'honour killings' and female genital mutilation are *absolutely unacceptable* to Trudeau, but not barbaric. Perhaps if Mr. Trudeau's private parts were carved up with broken glass he'd see it another way.

Justin Trudeau is not subjected to these absolutely unacceptable practices, though. Young women are. Young girls are.

Trudeau did backpedal a little after the initial uproar over his comments.

> *"We accept that these acts are absolutely unacceptable. That's not the debate. In casual conversation, I'd even use the word barbaric to describe female circumcision, for example, but in an official Government of Canada publication, there needs to be a little bit of an attempt at responsible neutrality."*

Justin Trudeau says the Government of Canada should not offend barbarians who carve up women's genitals.

I disagree. Immigration Minister Jason Kenney wouldn't stand for it either. He slammed Trudeau in this statement.

> *"Despite Trudeau's opposition, we make no apologies for letting immigrant women know their rights. We won't turn a blind eye to the abuse of immigrant women, even if the Ignatieff Liberals prefer we err on the side of political correctness."*

Social media vomited all over Justin Trudeau for his comments. He defended his position repeatedly but was mocked and ridiculed each and every time. Justin Trudeau finally admitted defeat and surrendered with this admission.

> *"Ok, final word: all violence against women is barbaric. If my concerns about language led some to think otherwise, then I gladly apologize."*

Liberal Party Leader Michael Ignatief unilaterally declared the matter closed with his pronouncement there is no such thing as honour killings.

> *"Let's not play word games with this stuff. Canada is based on equality between the sexes, equality of respect. There's no such thing as an 'honour' killing. There's only killing, and it's a crime everywhere."*

He issued a formal apology on March 15, 2011. Presumably someone sat Justin Trudeau down and explained how the world works.

> *"Perhaps I got tangled in semantic weeds in my comments, particularly in view of the Conservatives' cynicism on these issues. I want to make it clear that I think the acts described are heinous, barbaric acts that are totally unacceptable in our society."*

It took a long time, a social media and political firestorm and a good talking to from the Liberal Party brass to force Justin Trudeau to admit female genital mutilation is barbaric.

> *"...but in an official Government of Canada publication, there needs to be a little bit of an attempt at responsible neutrality."*

I don't want neutrality, responsible or otherwise, when it comes to mutilating human beings. I *want* to offend practitioners of spousal abuse, 'honour killings' and female genital mutilation. Yes, regardless of their religion or country of origin.

Trudeau's primary concern was for the hurt feelings of barbarians. His secondary concern was press coverage of his own political correctness and furthering the Trudeau brand. Protecting women from those who would mutilate their genitals?

For Canada's celebrity feminist, that came a distant third.

Does Justin Trudeau's feminist hypocrisy concern anyone?

"The Liberal Party of Canada does not discriminate"

Reggie Littlejohn, founder and president of *Women's Rights without Frontiers*, called Trudeau's pro-abortion stance hypocritical.

> *"Aborting a baby just because she is a girl is the ultimate act of gender discrimination. It says that women are so worthless they don't deserve to be born. No one can say that they stand for women's rights without standing against the sex-selective abortion of future women."*

In response, Liberal Policy Chair Maryanne Kampouris claimed:

> *"All Canadians, including Liberal Members of Parliament and candidates, are free to express their deeply held beliefs, and, more specifically the Liberal Party of Canada does not discriminate against current or potential candidates because of these beliefs."*

Except that's not true.

Not only will Justin Trudeau vet potential candidates for the Liberal Party of Canada he will also vet individual Party members.

> *"For current members, we will not eject someone from the party for beliefs they have long held. But the Liberal party is a pro-choice party, and going forward, all new members and new candidates are pro-choice."*

Perhaps I should purchase a Liberal Party Membership and see if he stamps DENIED on my application.

Before you are permitted to run as a Liberal candidate you must first clear the Liberal Party's Green Light Process. Then and only then are you free to speak your mind, and by "speak your mind" Justin Trudeau means you will parrot the opinions delivered to you from on high.

Dour consequences await anyone who fails to comply with this new edict from Trudeau's new open and transparent Liberal Party.

Back to Reggie Littlejohn's conclusion about our Prime Minister.

"To say that you stand for women's rights and, at the same time, to support the sex-selective abortion of future women is hypocrisy."

Indeed.

"Faithful Catholic" Justin Trudeau attends Planned Parenthood fundraiser

Justin Trudeau claims he is a faithful Catholic yet he actively supports and promotes abortion. He attends Planned Parenthood fundraisers and he refuses to condemn sex-selective abortion.

Justin Trudeau jumps onto his high moral horse despite his blatant hypocrisy. His outrage at anyone daring to question his Catholic faith is disingenuous as a result.

"Are there any tenets of the Catholic faith that Justin supports?"

Conservative MP Dean Del Mastro asked that question on Facebook and drew sharp comments from Trudeau in response.

On Tuesday, Trudeau said he was *"surprisingly upset"* that someone would question his faith and accuse him of being a *"bad Catholic."*

"My own personal faith is an extremely important part of who I am and the values that I try to lead with," he told the Canadian Press.

Justin Trudeau admits he does not support crucial pillars of the Catholic Church. It's no big deal. It's just politics.

"As a politician I have political positions on gay marriage and on abortion that don't at all resemble those of the Catholic Church."

"My own credo is completely consistent with that, and I'll defend my own faith and my own values to the utmost extent."

How Justin Trudeau can rationalize being upset at Del Mastro for questioning his Catholic faith is hard to comprehend. His unwavering support for abortion and same-sex marriage directly oppose fundamental tenets of Catholicism. This is the very definition of hypocrisy.

Justin Trudeau comes by this hypocrisy honestly, however. He learned it at the feet of his father, Pierre Elliot Trudeau.

Justin explains.

> *"I had an extraordinary example in a father who had deeply, deeply held personal views that were informed by the fact that he went to church every Sunday, read the Bible regularly to us, and raised us very, very religious, very Catholic, but at the same time he had no problem legalizing divorce, decriminalizing homosexuality and moving in ways that recognized the basic rights of the people."*

Justin ignores the fact his father led the pro-abortion movement and it was, in fact, Pierre Elliot Trudeau's Liberal government that legalized abortion in 1969 through the *Criminal Law Amendment Act, 1968-69.*

The hypocrisy and arrogance of Trudeau, both father and son, brings to mind a quote from Jess C. Scott:

"Hypocrites get offended by the truth."

No wonder Trudeau was so upset when Del Mastro questioned his Catholic faith.

Actual faithful Catholics are so appalled by Justin Trudeau's zeal for abortion they want to deny him communion and excommunicate him from the Roman Catholic Church.

Bishop Christian Riesbeck of Ottawa, May 8:

> *"Every person is called to stand for life. Although now we are told, as we heard in the news yesterday, that if you want to be an MP in the next election and you are pro-life you will be screened out and won't be allowed to run. So much for democracy!"*

Archbishop Terrence Prendergast of Ottawa, May 14:

"One may not dissent from these core teachings on life issues and be considered a Catholic in good standing. The position of the Catholic Church in favour of life at all stages is clear and unchanging.

A person who takes a position in contradiction to the teaching of the Catholic Church on the value and dignity of human life from the moment of conception to the moment of a natural death, and persists in this belief, is not in communion with the Church's values and teaching, which we believe faithfully transmit for today the teachings of Christ."

Archbishop Richard W. Smith of Edmonton, May 21:

"A pro-abortion stance is irreconcilable with Catholicism. Period."

On the May 21 edition of CBC Radio's *As It Happens* Bishop Christian Riesbeck of Ottawa gave his thoughts on Trudeau receiving communion:

"But, someone who persists — who obstinately persists — in teachings contrary to the clear and unchanging teachings on the core issues of life — if he obstinately persists in that — then, they can be denied Communion according to the Law of The Church."

Bishop Fred Henry of Calgary, May 21:

"[Trudeau] pledges open nomination races and at the same time: 'I have made it clear that future candidates need to be completely understanding that they will be expected to vote pro-choice on any bills.' Apparently, logic isn't his strong suit. [...] Regrettably, our Members of Parliament are content to play a political game with life refusing to even discuss the question. Furthermore, their cowardice and silence is inconsistent with scientific facts and places them in compliance with the destruction of thousands of human lives."

Faith Goldy was a reporter with *Sun News* in April 2014. She is also a proud Catholic. Goldy called for Justin Trudeau to be formally excommunicated from the Roman Catholic Church based on his pro-abortion fanaticism.

> *"Apart from being the drama teacher turned Liberal leader, Justin Trudeau is a self-professed Catholic and abortion extremist. By my read: that earns him the badges of heretic and excommunicant."*

Abortion is morally evil according to the Catholic Church because it violates the right to life of an innocent person, the unborn child.

American Cardinal Raymond Burke is a prominent canon lawyer and head of the Apostolic Signatura. He strengthens Faith Goldy's call for Justin Trudeau's excommunication.

> *"In the case of a politician or other public figure who acts against the moral law in a grave matter and yet presents himself to receive Holy Communion, the priest should admonish the person in question and then, if he or she persists in approaching to receive Holy Communion, the priest should refuse to give the Body of Christ to the person."*

I would love to see our Prime Minister excommunicated from the Roman Catholic Church.

We live in an age where honesty and integrity are irrelevant and antiquated concepts. In such an age excommunicating Canada's 23rd Prime Minister would send an impressive message to *mere citizens* and politicians alike.

****

What follows is Justin Trudeau at his best. He refuses to answer the question regardless of how delicately Marissa Semkiw asks it.

MARISSA SEMKIW: *"A woman comes to you. She says she's pregnant with a girl and she wants to terminate the life of the child because it's a girl. What would you say to her?"*

JUSTIN TRUDEAU: *"My position has been very clear. The Liberal Party is the party standing up for people's rights. And the Liberal Party will always be the party of the Charter. So we will continue to stand up for people's rights and not legislate them away."*

MARISSA SEMKIW: *"So to be clear, you wouldn't discourage her from having an abortion because it's a girl?"*

JUSTIN TRUDEAU: *"My role as the leader of the Liberal Party is to make sure that Canadian legislation respects people's rights and that's what I will continue to do."*

MARISSA SEMKIW: *"Yesterday you said you were happy with the status quo on abortion. But right now the status quo is that it's perfectly fine to abort a child because it's a girl. Do you have no qualms with that?"*

JUSTIN TRUDEAU: *"I will leave discussions like that between a woman and the health professionals that she encounters. I don't think the government should be in the business of legislating away people's rights. And that's why the Liberal Party is steadfast in this position."*

Justin Trudeau's Ethical Lobotomy on Abortion

"I don't know that there's anyone in this country that is in favor of abortions. But what I am very much in favor of is a woman's right to make that determination on her own, in consultation with the medical community, in consultation with whoever she chooses to consult. It is not for a room full of predominantly male legislators to take away those rights from women."

Justin Trudeau doesn't "know that there's anyone in this country in favour of abortions." Why does he zealously promote abortion in direct opposition of his professed Catholic beliefs? Why does he insist all Liberal candidates must be pro-abortion?

"I have made it clear that future candidates need to be completely understanding that they will be expected to vote pro-choice on any bills."

An MP that expresses a personal opinion on abortion? The very thought is anathema to him. This is now Justin Trudeau's Canada. You will do what you're told. Full stop.

But what about existing Liberal candidates or Members of Parliament? Will Trudeau allow them to vote their conscience or abstain from a vote on abortion?

> *"They must make concrete commitment to be openly pro-choice in their positions if they want to be a candidate in 2015."*

That's quite a decree from the man who called Stephen Harper dictatorial.

Rosie DiManno of the *Toronto Star* wrote the following to address Trudeau's ethical lobotomy on abortion.

> *"The irony of unintended consequences here is that all of a sudden abortion is back in the domain of public debate, which we could all have done without. Trudeau has opened that door by his absolute position. If you have doubts, if you have reservations -- moral, religious, any flicker of conscience -- then you're not wanted under the Liberal big tent and can't exercise, as an MP, a free vote should the matter arise in Parliament in any variation: sex selection abortions, for example, the termination of a female fetus because a boy-child is preferred, with some absolutist pro-choice feminists contorting themselves into intellectual pretzels, caving into gender-hatred disguised as cultural values rather than conceding an inch; late-term abortions, when the fetus is viable, because we're assured this is a rare occurrence, performed only when the mother's life is at risk."*

Canada's celebrity feminist also sees no conflict between his self-proclaimed feminism and his refusal to condemn killing babies just because they are female.

> *Marissa Semkiw: "Yesterday you said you were happy with the status quo on abortion. But right now the status quo is that it's perfectly fine to abort a child because it's a girl. Do you have no qualms with that?"*

Justin Trudeau: "I will leave discussions like that between a woman and the health professionals that she encounters."

Justin Trudeau finds no conflict between promoting abortion and his professed Roman Catholic faith either, despite repeated admonitions his pro-abortion stance violates basic tenets of the Catholic Church.

Justin Trudeau and Sex-Selective Abortion

"I am a feminist. I'm proud to be a feminist. I am a strong advocate for women's rights, and I'm not a woman."

There you have it. Justin Trudeau is a feminist. So why is he unwilling to stand against the heinous practice of sex-selective abortion?

That's the question he refuses to answer. When asked what he would say to a woman who wanted an abortion because her unborn child was female, Justin Trudeau said he would…

"…leave discussions like that between a woman and the health professionals that she encounters."

Canada's celebrity feminist abdicated his responsibility as a defender of women's rights. He refused to condemn killing unborn female babies for the crime of being female. Justin Trudeau is no feminist.

Conservative MP John Williamson is furious Trudeau will not condemn sex-selective abortion. In 2014 Williamson wrote an email to Sun News decrying Trudeau's bizarre refusal.

"The Liberal leader's refusal to condemn the awful practice of sex-selection abortion puts him far, far outside the mainstream of public opinion. When aborting girls just because they are girls doesn't cause Justin Trudeau to even question that decision or express any unease it is safe to say he is a pro-abortion fanatic."

The charge that Justin Trudeau is a pro-abortion fanatic holds up in light of his stance on Liberal Party candidates, Liberal MPs and their public positions on abortion.

> *"They must make concrete commitment to be openly pro-choice in their positions and if they want to be a candidate in 2015."*

Hypocrisy Alert.

A *true* feminist would never advocate killing an unborn baby simply because that baby is female.

Case closed.

Workplace Violence is Okay if You are Justin Trudeau

Liberals say workplace violence is bad, absolutely unacceptable even. Except when Liberal Prime Minister Justin Trudeau is the perpetrator of workplace violence. Then the good little sheep (we call them Liberal Members of Parliament) applaud Justin Trudeau's workplace violence with gusto. It's disgraceful.

We witnessed an impatient Prime Minister Trudeau stomp across the floor of Parliament and grab Conservative Party whip Gord Brown. He then dragged Brown away but not before he elbowed NDP MP Ruth Ellen Brosseau in the chest.

> *"The prime minister intentionally walked over, swore at us, reached between a few members of Parliament to grab the (Conservative) whip ... how did he think he wasn't going to hit anybody else?"*

Is this any way for a Prime Minister to speak in the House of Commons?

> *"Get the f*** out of the way."*

I think not.

Imagine the uproar if former Prime Minister Stephen Harper uttered those words instead of Justin Trudeau? The mainstream media would fillet The Greatest Enemy Canada Has Ever Known every hour on the hour.

But it wasn't Stephen Harper. The offender was Prime Minister Justin Trudeau so the media dutifully ignored it as best they could.

Move along. Nothing to see here folks, insisted our Media Party lapdogs.

Interim Conservative Leader Rona Ambrose:

> *"His behaviour was unbecoming of a leader who has the privilege, and let's never forget it's a privilege, bestowed on him by the people of Canada to sit as prime minister in this place. Everything he did from the moment he left his seat was unnecessary and it was unsettling."*

There is no excuse for the ensuing temper tantrum from our Prime Minister. Trudeau's actions are those of a petulant child told "No." Trudeau's absurd rationalization for his behaviour is laughable.

> *"The opposition whip seemed to be impeded with his progress. In so doing, I admit I came into physical contact with a number of members."*

Had a Conservative MP elbowed Ruth Ellen Brosseau in the chest the Liberal Party would call for a national inquiry and demand the guilty party resign their seat. Had a Conservative Prime Minister done so I cannot even imagine the outrage. The Liberal Party uproar would be epic.

While I do not agree with Thomas Mulcair on a great many issues, on this he and I see eye to eye. I applaud Mr. Mulcair for defending his MP.

> *"What kind of man elbows a woman? It's pathetic. You're pathetic."*

All Justin Trudeau could say for himself was this.

> *"I completely apologize. It was not my intention to hurt anyone."*

That's the thing about intentions. They're flawless. Always. Our actions, however, reveal our true character, as unpleasant as that may be. It is not what we say that matters, but what we do.

Politicians, like the *mere citizens* they claim to represent, should be judged by their actions, not their intentions.

What follows is not the sanitized and coherent version of his speech served up by the mainstream media. I transcribed this verbatim and present his *actual* speech instead.

> *"Uh, I want to, uh, take the opportunity, uh, now that the Member has, uh, is ah, is okay to return to the House right now, uh, to be able to express directly to her, uh, my apologies, uh, for my behaviour and my actions. Unreservedly. The fact is, un, in, uh, this situation where I saw... No! I'm not... Explanations... Mr. Speaker... I.... I noticed... that the, uh, member, uh, the opposite uh member whip, uh, was being impeded in his progress. I... took it upon myself, uh, to assist him forward, uh, which was, which was I now see, uh, unadviseable as a course of actions, uh, and resulted in, uh, physical contact in this house, uh, that, uh, we can all accept was, uh, un... un... un... unacceptable and I apologize for that unreservedly, uh, and I look for opportunities, uh, to make amends, uh, directly to the member, uh, and to any members, uh, who, uh, feel, uh, negatively impacted, uh, by this, uh, by this, uh, exchange and intervention, uh, because I take responsibility."*

It's embarrassing our Prime Minister cannot speak half a dozen syllables without fumbling for more words.

Even more embarrassing is the video of his apology in the House of Commons. His insincerity is palpable. He can barely keep the smirk off his face.

It takes a big man to face the woman you wronged and apologize.

His refusal to apologize to Ms. Brosseau in person reveals Justin Trudeau's feminism for what it really is: an affectation to garner votes, a veneer, not a deeply held personal belief.

A true feminist would do the right thing. A true feminist would apologize to the woman he hurt, in person and out of sight of video cameras.

Not Justin Trudeau.

He did apologize but not directly to Ruth Ellen Brosseau and only when television cameras pointed his way.

We learned a lot about the character of our Prime Minister today. What we learned is deeply troubling and, dare I say it, disgraceful.

Justin Trudeau's Flip-Flop on Guns

When Justin was just an MP in the House of Commons he proudly voted to keep Canada's failed gun registry. Once he became leader of the Liberal Party he took an entirely different position on guns.

Justin Trudeau is now both for and against the Gun Registry.

In English Canada he opposes the long gun registry.

> *"The long-gun registry, as it was, was a failure and I'm not going to resuscitate that."*

In French Canada he's totally for it.

> *"I find it's a very good idea. Because in Quebec it was not at all as divisive as it was elsewhere in the country."*

Flip...flop...flip...flop.

Justin Trudeau believes in different laws for different Canadians too.

> *"Perhaps a solution is to let provinces find different solutions. What's important is protecting Quebecers from gun violence."*

What's important is protecting Quebecers?

Not Canadians. Justin Trudeau is first, foremost and always a Quebecer, not a Canadian.

While Mr. Trudeau says he won't register guns, his personal gun control Senator Celine Hervieux-Payette explains otherwise.

"I developed Bill S-231 around the idea that all firearms should be prohibited except those used in sport shooting..."

The Liberal Party of Canada prefers to ban firearms, not register them. Disingenuously titled *Strengthening Canadians' Security and Promoting Hunting and Recreational Shooting Act*, Senate Bill S-231 would:

o   Prohibit all firearms in Canada except hunting firearms;
o   limit the definition of hunting firearms...;
o   limit the transport of circumscribed firearms to transporters, thus controlling the movement of firearms in Canada; and
o   undo all the provisions of Bill C-42, except for the prohibition on obtaining a licence to possess and acquire firearms following a domestic violence conviction.

Trudeau would change the classification of certain firearms to ban them in Canada. He would then review firearm licences and revoke those he deemed unacceptable.

"There are many different ways, jurisdictions around the world are looking into gun control. A lot can be done around classification [of firearms], a lot can be done around proper review of people wishing to ... purchase firearms."

Justin Trudeau, given half a chance, would review responsible firearms ownership out of existence. The only thing gun owners need to remember about Justin Trudeau is this:

"I voted to keep the firearms registry a few months ago and if we had a vote tomorrow I would vote once again to keep the long-gun registry."

Repeal Mandatory Minimum Sentences for Pedophiles

QUESTION: *"Would you rule out repealing mandatory minimums for sexual crimes against children?"*

TRUDEAU: *"No, I wouldn't rule out repealing mandatory minimums for anyone."*

Former Conservative Public Safety Minister Vic Toews famously said Canadians *stand with us or with the child pornographers*.

Justin Trudeau confirmed he wouldn't rule out repealing mandatory minimums for child molesters. He also confirmed he stands, using Vic Toews' vernacular, with the child pornographers.

That ought to terrify every single Canadian parent. The Conservative government raised many mandatory minimum sentences for a good reason. Canadian judges love the *hug-a-thug* approach to sentencing even the most heinous offenders, including child molesters.

For example, in 2009 Hai Binh Nghiem was convicted for attempting to sexually assault two elementary school girls, one in 2006 and the other in 2007.

His sentence? Nine months for each sexual assault, to be served consecutively. Hai Binh Nghiem then took exception to the trial judge referring to him as an *untreated sexual predator* and appealed his already soft sentence.

That's just one example. If you search the Canadian Legal Information Institute database (canlii.org) you will find hundreds more just like it.

There is a reason we need mandatory minimum sentences for child molesters. Our judges will not remove them from society any other way.

Lorne Gunter wrote in the *Edmonton Sun*:

> *"The Tories have upped the minimums for impaired driving after watching too many killer drunks get off lightly. They've upped the minimums for white-collar crooks, serial car thieves, drive-by shooters, human traffickers, operators of meth labs and large-scale grow-ops, kidnappers and those who peddle drugs to kids.*
>
> *There's very little to object to in that list."*

Unless you are Justin Trudeau, leader of the Liberal Party of Canada.

Then you object to all of it.

"Being convicted of a sex-related offence in Canada will not necessarily result in a federal sentence (i.e., two years or more). Individuals who are incarcerated for sex-related offences are more likely to be committed to provincial facilities for a period of less than two years."

— Corrections Canada Website

Security, Foreign Affairs / Terrorism

The Temporary Foreign Worker Program

"Most concerning, the [Temporary Foreign Workers] program has grown dramatically in regions facing high unemployment, like southwestern Ontario. In Windsor, the number of unemployed workers has risen by 40 per cent while the number of foreign workers in the city has grown by 86 per cent. Unemployment in London has risen by 27 per cent while the number of foreign workers has increased by 87 per cent."

In a May 5, 2014 *Toronto Star* editorial Justin Trudeau railed against the Temporary Foreign Workers program and the Conservative government's supposed mismanagement of it. He offered the following advice on how to fix a program he clearly dislikes.

"First, the Temporary Foreign Worker Program needs to be scaled back dramatically over time, and refocused on its original purpose: to fill jobs on a limited basis when no Canadian workers can be found.

Second, Canada needs to re-commit itself to bringing permanent immigrants here who have a path to citizenship. This would return us back to first principles and the purpose of immigration: nation building.

Third, we must also create real transparency and accountability in the program. This should begin with a full review of the program by the Auditor General. We must tighten the foreign worker approvals process, through the disclosure of applications and approvals of temporary foreign workers. This can be facilitated with the public disclosure of information concerning what jobs are being offered to temporary foreign workers and in what communities.

Fourth, we must require that employers applying to the program have clearly attempted to fill job vacancies with Canadian workers, particularly young Canadians whose unemployment rate is nearly twice the national average. We require Canadians who are collecting EI benefits to prove they are looking for work.

It's only fair that we require employers looking to benefit from the Temporary Foreign Worker Program to prove they really need it.

Finally, the government should tighten the Labour Market Opinion approval process to ensure that only businesses with legitimate needs are able to access the program."

There is one small problem with Trudeau's public contempt. He personally hired a nanny through the Temporary Foreign Workers Program.

He also petitioned the program for restaurant workers from China on behalf of a high-end Papineau eatery frequented by his father.

That Trudeau's hypocrisy bubbled to the surface here surprised no one.

Olivier Duchesneau, Trudeau's deputy director of communications, offered this explanation:

"Mr. Trudeau and Ms. Grégoire Trudeau submitted one successful application to the temporary foreign worker program for a caregiver, prior to Mr. Trudeau becoming the leader of the Liberal Party. Employment with this individual ceased before Mr. Trudeau became leader of the Liberal Party."

Justin Trudeau's "do as I say not as I do" attitude is wearing pretty thin.

We're only in Year One of his imperious reign over Canadians.

If Trudeau's hypocrisy is this blatant already can you imagine how offensive it will be in four years?

We will repeal the parts that are problematic with C-51

"You won't hear me say, 'Mr. Mulcair, who voted against physical security doesn't care about Canadians' safety.' And yes, it's a position that is more easily attacked than the other positions are. But it's also the right position. Because we are in a position of saying we will do both. We will protect Canadians' physical security and uphold their rights and freedoms by demonstrating that we will repeal the parts that are problematic with C-51. We will bring in proper oversight. We will bring in a review clause for three years so that we, as the Liberal party has done in the past in the years following 9/11, both defend peoples' physical security and protect their rights and freedoms."

Justin Trudeau promised to repeal the problematic sections of Bill C-51. He reiterated this throughout the 2015 election campaign. How fast would he make those changes if elected?

"As quickly as is possible. There's going to be a lot to do if we form government, but it will be one of those priorities. Because Canadians have expressed very clearly that they want both their physical security and their rights upheld.

And as the party of the Charter, as the party that has always understood how important peoples' rights and freedoms are, as someone who has demonstrated it on a wide range of issues throughout my leadership, we will move on it very quickly."

Prime Minister Trudeau hasn't lifted a finger to keep his campaign promise. His only action? He appointed Liberal MP David McGuinty to study the issue.

Before he voted in favour, Justin Trudeau announced Bill C-51 would never pass without Liberal amendments.

He greatly overstated his power to influence. Bill C-51 passed as written despite heavy opposition from the *mere citizens* of Canada.

Monia Mazigh, writing for *Huffington Post*, explained Canadians' opposition to the intrusive act.

> *"Canadians did not want more powers to be given to security intelligence forces, they didn't want to restrict their freedom of expression and dissent, they didn't want their information to be shared with 17 federal agencies, they didn't want Canadian judges to violate the Charter and allow intelligence officers enter their home or seize their laptops without a judicial warrant."*

Canadians' awareness of C-51 consistently hovered around 70%. Awareness among Liberal supporters was even higher at 79%. Disapproval of the legislation ran 56% nationwide but an astonishing 75% in youth according to a *Forum Research* poll.

> *"It appears that the more Canadians learn about Bill C51, the less they like it. The need for the bill is seen to be diminishing, and voters recognize some provisions may impact on their lives in ways they don't like. With an election approaching, the government would be well-advised to determine whether this bill is the hill they want to stake themselves out on,"* said Forum Research President, Dr. Lorne Bozinoff.

Political commentators referred to Justin Trudeau's defense of our Charter rights while passing legislation that violates those Charter rights as *pretzel logic.*

Trudeau saw no issue with holding two contradictory positions. He called out Prime Minister Stephen Harper for not doing enough to defend Canadians' rights and freedoms. At the same time he attacked NDP Leader Thomas Mulcair for not doing enough to protect Canadians' national security.

> *"Mr. Harper doesn't think we need to do anything more to defend our rights and freedoms. Mr. Mulcair doesn't think we need to do anything more to protect our national security. We need to make sure we are doing both those things, together."*

Pretzel logic.

One of the biggest issues with Bill C-51, the *Anti-Terrorism Act 2015* as it is now known, is the ability of government departments to share more personal information with each other.

Bill C-51 made these changes to the *Security of Canada Information Sharing Act* and affect anyone the government deems a threat. Who the government deems a threat is open to debate. It is purposefully not defined in the Act.

Could my disapproval of Justin Trudeau's contradictory statements and actions earn me that designation?

It is entirely possible. I'd bet it's even probable. There is no credible oversight of Canada's security services. We will not know for sure until the Canadian government designates someone a threat and deals with them as such.

While in opposition Trudeau railed against many aspects of Bill C-51. Now that he is Prime Minister those former objections are a distant memory. So much for his assurance he *will move on it very quickly.*

Andrew Mitrovica, writing for *iPolitics.ca*, highlighted Trudeau's statement on security and charter rights in his inaugural throne speech. Mitrovica made a great point about Trudeau's lack of movement on C-51.

> *"If the Liberals intended to repeal C-51, they would have said so. If they'd intended to repeal large parts of the law, they would have sent some signals by now. If they haven't, common sense suggests it's because Trudeau has chosen to leave C-51 largely intact. And the strongest indication yet that C-51 is going to emerge relatively unscathed from Trudeau's first year in power is his cockeyed decision to keep on ex-CSIS director Richard Fadden as his national security adviser."*

Now that Justin Trudeau sits in the Prime Minister's Office he wants all the powers he opposed when in opposition. The relaxed restrictions on who police can arrest without a warrant is, no doubt, a section of legislation Canada's 23rd Prime Minister finds particularly appealing.

Canadian Journalists for Free Expression find Trudeau's complacency thoroughly unacceptable.

> *"Nothing has changed since over 300,000 Canadians called for a full repeal, marched in the streets and made their voices heard to speak out against this legislation. Stephen Harper may be gone but Bill C-51 is still the law of the land.*
>
> *Prime Minister Justin Trudeau has promised to amend the bill to remove the 'problematic elements', but nothing has been done yet. CJFE is meeting with Ministers and MPs to actively engage for real reform that will protect our constitutional rights, but voices within the security services are relentlessly working behind the scenes to water down any changes. They're betting that Canadians have forgotten about this issue."*

That is precisely what Liberals are counting on.

In his Throne Speech Justin Trudeau claimed to defend the very Charter rights he stripped from us when he voted for Bill C-51.

> *"Recognizing that Canada is, fundamentally, a safe and peaceful country, the Government will continue to work to keep all Canadians safe, while at the same time protecting our cherished rights and freedoms."*

Pretzel logic.

Did you honestly expect anything different from the man who delivers Pablum and calls it a Throne Speech?

Justin Trudeau's Visits *"Stone Them to Death"* Imam

Justin Trudeau showed an appalling lack of judgment when he chose to visit Imam Foudil Selmoune, a Montreal Muslim cleric who publicly advocates stoning people to death.

Selmoune advocates Sharia law in Canada. He wants Canadian Muslims ruled, not by Canadian law and Canadian courts, but by Sharia law and Sharia courts.

Equality for all? Such a silly, outdated western notion.

Imam Foudil Selmoune spoke to Radio Canada and said stoning was merely a part of God's rules so Muslims can live in a peaceful and just society.

> *"We don't cut hands off just anyone,"* he said. *"We cut the hands of people who have money and who steal."*

At least Selmoune has specific criteria for whose hands to cut off.

> *"people who have money and who steal"*

Should Selmoune get his way Canada would have one law for Muslims and another for kafirs (non-believers or infidels). That means the rest of us.

But a penchant for stoning *people who have money and who steal* isn't the biggest problem with Imam Foudil Selmoune, if you can believe it.

This Imam, or at least the Brossard Islamic Community Centre he runs, sent over $11,000 to IRFAN-Canada, a former charity now listed as a terrorist entity by the Canadian government. IRFAN-Canada's charitable status was revoked.

Imam Foudil Selmoune claims no knowledge of terrorist ties to IRFAN-Canada, of course, and is emphatic his mosque cannot be condemned for funding the group before it was discovered to be a terror-supporting front.

Let's examine one case that shines the light of doubt on Selmoune's claim.

One of Brossard Islamic Community Centre's regular attendees, Misbahuddin Ahmed, was sentenced to 12 years in prison for his conviction of conspiracy to facilitate a terrorist offence and facilitating a terrorist offence. These crimes carry maximum punishments of up to 14 years imprisonment for the first charge and up to 10 years of imprisonment for the second.

He was acquitted of a third charge, possessing explosive substances with intent to endanger life or cause serious damage to property for the benefit of or at the direction of, or in association with a terrorist group.

Justice Colin McKinnon wrote the following when sentencing Ahmen.

*"The decision of the court is that Mr. Ahmed will be
sentenced to a term in penitentiary of 12 years, 5 years
for conspiracy and 7 years consecutive for
participating in the activities of a terrorist group. In
my view, the length of this sentence accords with the
gravity of Mr. Ahmed's conduct, and provides
adequate denunciation of his crimes, and deterrence
for those who would contemplate similar actions.*

*In addition, a 12 year sentence reflects Mr. Ahmed's
lesser moral culpability as compared to Mr.
Alizadeh's, and accords with the sentences given to the
camp plot members of the Toronto 18, as well as the
Court of Appeal's decisions in Gaya and Khalid, and
the Supreme Court's decision in Khawaja. I find that a
12 year sentence also satisfies the totality principle, as
it is proportionate to Mr. Ahmed's culpability in
committing these serious offences."*

Justin Trudeau thinks a radical Islamic Mosque with proven ties to
terrorism is an appropriate venue for a campaign visit. That decision
speaks volumes about Justin Trudeau's character, leadership and political
priorities.

That decision ought to concern to every Canadian.

Trudeau and the Reviving Islamic Spirit Convention

*"The Reviving the Islamic Spirit [RIS] convention… is
also about celebrating our shared beliefs in justice,
fairness, equality of opportunity and acceptance. The
work you do in communities across the country is what
builds the [sic] and strengthens our multicultural
fabric."*

Prime Minister Trudeau delivered this message to the Reviving Islamic
Spirit convention held in Toronto from December 25-27, 2015.

His fondness for Muslims is well documented.

I, however, am baffled by it. Here's why.

The followers of Islam have no use or desire for Canada's multicultural fabric. A cursory examination of a textbook sold during the convention, "Islamic Studies" by Husain A. Nuri and Mansur Aham, makes that abundantly clear.

> *p. 79*
> *"...her [the woman's] legal liabilities are equal to man's liabilities. If she commits an offence, her penalty is no less or no more than a man's penalty in a similar case. For the crime of adultery, her punishment is 100 stripes, the same for a man..."*

This is far better than the former position that required the woman to be stoned to death. This new position expresses equality for men and women. Fantastic.

> *p. 85*
> *"Islam allows a Muslim man to marry a Jewish or Christian woman...Islam has prohibited Muslim women from marrying non-Muslim men..."*

Despite their commitment to equality of punishment for adultery, that equality does not extend to a choice of marriage partners. That's okay. I'm sure Justin will modify the Canadian Charter of Rights and Freedoms to reflect this new multicultural fabric Islam brings to Canada.

> *p. 87*
> *"While Islamic ethics advocates strict monogamy, Islam has allowed a Muslim man to marry up to four women. However, a Muslim man can have multiple wives only if [sic] under certain obligations, and provided that he meets certain conditions."*
> *[verbatim]*

This can't even make sense to Justin Trudeau. Or maybe it can. I suppose one parallel is Justin's claim he is a devout Roman Catholic while dogmatically supporting abortion and same-sex marriage in direct opposition to that Catholic faith.

> *P. 98*
> *"In many Islamic writings, the word khalifah is understood as a political system. The title khalifah is used for the leader of the Islamic world. The leader*

has the right to adopt the divine rules, protect the religion, and rule the Islamic world. Thus all the leaders after Rasul [messanger] Muhammad (S) where political successors to Rasulullah [messenger of Allah] (S), therefore, known as khalifah. A Caliph or Khalifah is recognized as the Amir al-Mu'minin, or the Commander of the Faithful.

More of the beautiful multicultural fabric Islam brings to Canada. Justin Trudeau already bows down to Islam. It shouldn't be long before he makes Canada's subjection to Islam official. As soon as he announces Canada's Islamic Nation status Justin Trudeau will surely hand over the Prime Minister's office to the leader of Islamic world too.

P. 99
"In the seventh century, Islam provided mankind the ideal code of human rights. These rights conferred honour and dignity to mankind and eliminated oppression, exploitation, intimidation, coercion and injustice. Allah is the ultimate provider of law and He is the source of all human rights. Establishing and upholding human rights is integral to overall Islamic order. Thus, it is obligatory for Muslim government and rulers to implement human rights in true Islamic spirit. Therefore, no ruler, government or king should curtail or violate the human rights conferred by Allah...

Justin Trudeau is right. I'm convinced. Islam is thoroughly compatible with western values, traditions and government.

I have only one question. On what date will Justin Trudeau declare Canada's subservience to Sharia law and abdicate the Prime Minister's Office?

Trudeau's Terrorist Apologetics

"No question that this happened because there is someone who feels completely excluded, completely at war with innocents, at war with a society. And our approach has to be, OK, where do those tensions come from?"

This was Justin Trudeau's response to the horrific bombings at the Boston Marathon carried out by Muslim terrorists in April 2013.

He offered his own scrambled rationalization for why evil men do evil things but could not find it in his heart to condemn the act of terror that killed 3 people and injured 170 more.

He insisted terrorists are simply misunderstood. If we would just listen to their feelings perhaps these terrorists would kill less and love more.

What hogwash.

Contrast Trudeau's terrorist-loving Pablum with Stephen Harper's clear message.

> *"When you see this kind of violent act, you do not sit around trying to rationalize it or make excuses for it or figure out its root causes. You condemn it categorically."*

Four simple words from Stephen Harper say what must be said.

> *"You condemn it categorically."*

When Stephen Harper returned from London he explained further.

> *"I don't think we want to convey any view to the Canadian public other than our utter condemnation of this kind of violence."*

Canadians want two things when terrorists attack and kill innocent people. We want those heinous actions condemned in the strongest possible manner. We want our government's assurance it is doing everything in its power to prevent future terrorist acts from taking place.

Trudeau offered neither.

Condemning terrorists isn't the Trudeau way. He prefers to play "hug-a-terrorist" and pontificate about why they feel excluded.

Then came home-grown terrorist Aaron Driver. Thankfully security forces killed Driver as he left his home to plant and detonate his homemade bombs.

Paul Wells, in his column in the *Toronto Star*, pointed out that Prime Minister Trudeau did not address the nation about Aaron Driver's terrorism.

That task fell to Public Safety Minister Ralph Goodale, who slyly issued a press release on a long weekend. Trudeau's terrorist apologetics seeped into that press release, regardless.

> *"We have also budgeted for a new national office and centre of excellence for community outreach and counter-radicalization. We need to get really good at this -- to preserve our diversity and pluralism as unique national strengths."*

The Trudeau plan to stop home-grown terrorists like Aaron Driver? Counseling and intervention services. No, that's not a joke. Well yes, it is a joke, but that is Trudeau's plan.

Our liberty-defending Liberals will open an Office of Counter-Radicalization so we can put these poor misunderstood jihadists on the therapy couch.

Ralph Goodale also admitted a huge problem exists with the enforcement of peace bonds.

> *"(Driver's peace bond) is obviously a lesson that one needs to look at very carefully and we are examining very carefully what we need to do to make our police and security activity more effective."*

In other words, peace bonds aren't worth the paper they are printed on.

Is it possible the Liberal Party of Canada will finally comprehend criminals, those individuals intent upon committing evil acts, will never follow laws, will never follow peace bonds or restraining orders?

Those Liberals... they're mighty slow learners. We law-abiding gun owners have explained this simple truth to them for generations.

But let's get back to Justin Trudeau's statement on Aaron Driver. Surely the Prime Minister had something to say, right?

Uh, no. Not a peep.

Prime Minister Justin Trudeau was far too busy photo-bombing an unsuspecting couple's wedding in Tofino to address a national security concern or, for that matter, to act like a Prime Minister in any tangible way.

Justin Trudeau's full answer on Boston bombing terrorists

"First thing you offer support and sympathy and condolences, and can we send down EMTs, as we contributed after 9/11. I mean, is there any material, immediate support we can offer. And then at the same time, over the coming days, we have to look at the root causes.

Now, we don't know now whether it was terrorism or a single crazy, or a domestic issue or a foreign issue. But there is no question that this happened because there is someone who feels completely excluded, completely at war with innocents, at war with a society. And our approach has to be, okay, where do those tensions come from?

Yes, we have to make sure that we're promoting security and we're keeping our borders safe, and monitoring the kinds of violent subgroups that happen around. But we also have to monitor and encourage people to not point fingers at each other and lay blame for personal ills or societal ills on a specific group, whether it be the West or the government, or Bostonians, or whatever it is.

Because it's that idea of dividing humans against ourselves, pointing out that they're not like us, and in order to achieve political goals we can kill innocents here--that's something that no society in the world that is healthy, regardless of ideology, will accept.

Of course, I'd be worried about what specific targets there are. But there will always be more targets, more shopping centres, more public events, more gatherings than we can evacuate or we can deal with.

Yes, there is a need for security and response and being proactive and making sure that we have information. But we also need to make sure that as we go forward that we don't emphasize a culture of fear and mistrust, because that ends up marginalizing even further people who are already feeling like they are enemies of society rather than people who have hope for the future and faith that we can work together and succeed."

Convicted Terrorists Keep Your Passports

"And I'll give you the quote so that you guys can jot it down and put it in an attack ad somewhere that the Liberal Party believes that terrorists should get to keep their Canadian citizenship. Because I do. And I'm willing to take on anyone who disagrees with that."

Justin Trudeau insists terrorists should keep their Canadian citizenship. Can you think of a single valid reason why a convicted terrorist should keep his or her Canadian citizenship? Me neither. It defies common sense.

There are consequences for Canadian citizens who commit terrorist acts. In the case of a dual citizen convicted of terrorism, being stripped of their Canadian citizenship must be one of those consequences.

Not so, says Prime Minister Justin Trudeau.

"I think that a lot of Canadians, including very conservative Canadians, should be worried about the state willing to, and taking the power to, arbitrarily remove citizenship from people. That's a slippery slope that I don't think we want to go on."

Were that power arbitrary, as Trudeau contends then yes, I would agree. But that is not the case. Not even close.

When an individual is convicted of a terrorist act in a court of law then, and only then, can they be stripped of their citizenship.

That's no slippery slope. That's due process.

You'll never get Prime Minister Justin Trudeau to admit that, of course.

He despises those pesky little things called facts.

Is Brad Wall promoting hatred against Muslims?

Will Saskatchewan Premier Brad Wall face charges for promoting hatred against Islam? That idea is not as far-fetched as you might think after the National Council of Canadian Muslims (NCCM) released its anti-Islamophobia Charter.

The Liberal Party of Canada passed a resolution to officially condemn all forms of Islamophobia. It also called for the creation of a "Task Force for the Elimination of All Forms of Islamophobia." That task force would augment "Canada's strategic vision to eliminate all forms of discrimination and hatred."

What's this got to do with Saskatchewan Premier Brad Wall? Well, everything, actually.

On November 16, 2015 Premier Brad Wall wrote Canada's newly-elected Prime Minister a letter. He asked Justin Trudeau to reconsider his year-end deadline to bring in 25,000 Syrian refugees. Premier Wall expressed his concern over fast-tracking so many refugees.

> *"I am writing to raise Saskatchewan's concerns about the fast-tracking of refugee claims in order to meet your goal of bringing 25,000 Syrian refugees to Canada by the end of the year. I am concerned that the current date-driven plan could severely undermine the refugee screening process."*

That is a valid concern shared by millions of Canadians across the country.

This isn't about an unwillingness to help. It's about making sure we don't import terrorists based on an arbitrary deadline that does not allow enough time for adequate security screening.

> *"However, if even a small number of individuals who wish to do harm to our country are able to enter Canada as a result of a rushed refugee resettlement process, the results could be devastating. The recent attacks in Paris are a grim reminder of the death and destruction even a small number of malevolent individuals can inflict upon a peaceful country and its citizens.*

> *Surely, we do not want to be date-driven or numbers-driven in an endeavour that may affect the safety of our citizens and the security of our country."*

Brad Wall's concern is for the safety and security of Canadians. The usual circus freaks (they call themselves mainstream media reporters) immediately branded the Saskatchewan Premier an Islamophobe.

Former Liberal Immigration Minister Lloyd Axworthy also wasted no time lambasting Premier Wall. He did so in that bastion of unbiased news reporting, the CBC.

> *"I don't know why a premier would feel empowered to make that kind of request when he really doesn't have the information, doesn't really have the know-how ... to be able to assess what are the threats and risks in the area of refugees."*

Premier Wall is empowered by something both Axworthy and Trudeau lack: common sense.

As *Maclean's Magazine* noted in the wake of the Paris attacks, properly vetting immigrants is mandatory.

> *"Ahmad al Mohammad--if that's indeed his real name; no one's certain just yet--died a suicide bomber, blasting himself to pieces outside France's national soccer stadium on Friday night. Three days later, the photo ID he left behind at the crime scene has proven almost as damaging as his bomb.*

> *Lying near Mohammad's mangled body, investigators found a Syrian passport that chronicled a refugee's journey through Greece, Croatia and eventually to France--proof, it appeared, that the so-called Islamic State had exploited the migrant crisis to smuggle an operative into the West. The terrorist group had long warned of deploying such a tactic, and security experts had every reason to fear such a claim could come true."*

Unfortunately, vetting immigrants is not a security imperative for Justin Trudeau. Goodness no! He'd miss his all-important selfie deadline.

Remember, this same Prime Minister decreed Muslim dual citizens convicted of terrorist acts could not be stripped of their Canadian citizenship.

The fruits of the Liberal Party resolution I mentioned at the outset are now upon us. The National Council of Canadian Muslims (NCCM) proudly announced its anti-Islamophobia Charter, known by its full title *The Charter for Inclusive Communities.*

"Inclusive" is an interesting word choice.

As Tarek Fatah noted in his May 24, 2016 column, inclusiveness does not interest Muslim imams in Canada. Far from it, in fact, yet nobody brands them racists or a hate-mongers.

> *"For example, in a sermon on Friday, May 6 delivered at a mosque in Edmonton, an imam invoked the memory of Prophet Muhammad to whip up hatred against Israel.*
>
> *He declared peace accords with Israel are 'useless garbage,' and vowed 'Jerusalem will be conquered through blood.'*
>
> *In February, the same cleric predicted Islam would soon conquer Rome, 'the heart of the Christian state.'*
>
> *The Edmonton mosque diatribe was not isolated.*
>
> *On May 13, just north of Toronto, an Islamic society hosted a celebration of Iranian mass murderer, Ayatollah Khomeini. The poster promoting the event described Khomeini as a, 'Liberator and Reformer of the Masses.'*
>
> *On Saturday, the Islamist group Hizb-ut-Tahrir, banned in some countries, hosted a conference to discuss the re-establishment of a global Islamic caliphate."*

Brad Wall had the courage to speak the truth. That courage should be embraced, not just in Brad Wall but in every Canadian, not shouted down with catcalls of Islamophobe and racist.

How long until Saskatchewan Premier Brad Wall is hauled before the Canadian Human Rights Commission for discriminating against Muslims?

How long until Saskatchewan Premier Brad Wall faces criminal charges under Canada's hate crime provisions, Section 319 of the Criminal Code of Canada?

The answer probably depends on when Justin Trudeau is finished doling out billions of Canadian tax dollars on his Selfie World Tour.

Remind me, please, as I seem to have forgotten. How many Christians, Jews and Atheists flew planes into buildings in New York City on September 11th, 2001?

There is a reason Brad Wall expressed concern. His concern should be taken seriously by our Prime Minister, not ignored in favour of yet another selfie.

Let's Whip out our CF-18s

> *"Why aren't we talking more about the kind of humanitarian aid that Canada can and must be engaged in, rather than trying to whip out our CF-18s and show them how big they are? It just doesn't work like that in Canada."*

Justin Trudeau delivered that infantile sexual quip after his keynote speech to *Canada 2020*, a progressive think tank. Jason Kenny was quick to attack.

> *"Remarkable that Justin Trudeau uses juvenile humour (whip it out) to describe the use of force in combating genocide. Is this how Prime Minister Justin Trudeau would conduct himself in discussing use of air power at a NATO summit?"*

Prime Minister Harper's spokesman Jason MacDonald also issued a sharp criticism of Trudeau.

> *"Mr. Trudeau's comments are disrespectful of the Canadian Armed Forces and make light of a serious issue. Our involvement in the fight against ISIL is, and has been,*

motivated by a desire to do our part in fighting a group that has made direct terrorist threats against Canada and Canadians, in addition to carrying out atrocities against children, women, and men in the region. As the Prime Minister has said: 'we take that seriously and will do our part.'"

Justin Trudeau has no interest in combating terrorism. He prefers childish sound bites and the condemnation of others. He sits quietly on the sidelines ignoring terrorism and genocide committed by Muslim terrorists.

Canadians expect more from the man holding the highest office in the land. Sadly, we are destined for a great deal more disappointment over the next four years.

I Admire China's Basic Dictatorship

The Question: *"Which nation, besides Canada, which nation's administration do you most admire, and why?"*

"You know, there's a level of admiration I actually have for China because their basic dictatorship is allowing them to actually turn their economy around on a dime and say 'we need to go green fastest . . . we need to start investing in solar.' I mean there is a flexibility that I know Stephen Harper must dream about of having a dictatorship that he can do everything he wanted that I find quite interesting."

It says a lot about a man when he openly admires a communist dictatorship with an atrocious record on human rights.

It says even more about that man when he falsifies their commitment to green energy to rationalize his admiration. In 2016 China broke ground on new coal power plant construction sites at the rate of two per week. That's some commitment to green energy.

Justin Trudeau's belief China is going green is delusional.

Now imagine the Chinese government Justin Trudeau admires is the same government that imprisoned and tortured you.

Would his gushing admiration for your torturers build your faith in Justin Trudeau? Not a chance.

"Can I use the word 'foolish'?" asked one member of the Federation for a Democratic China.

"It seems to be that he's not well-informed," said another.

Foolish and uninformed are understatements.

Globe and Mail columnist Margaret Wente nailed it in her column on Trudeau's statements at a Ladies Night fundraising event.

> *"Justin's biggest political problem is that he looks vapid and lightweight. The trouble is, whenever he takes a stab at saying something really substantive, he winds up looking ... vapid and lightweight. That's a problem. Even when he's only talking to the ladies."*

Vapid and lightweight are great qualities in a leader, aren't they?

Justin Trudeau on Fidel Castro an International Laughing Stock

> *"It is with deep sorrow that I learned today of the death of Cuba's longest serving President. Fidel Castro was a larger than life leader who served his people for almost half a century. A legendary revolutionary and orator, Mr. Castro made significant improvements to the education and healthcare of his island nation.*
>
> *While a controversial figure, both Mr. Castro's supporters and detractors recognized his tremendous dedication and love for the Cuban people who had a deep and lasting affection for "el Comandante".*
>
> *I know my father was very proud to call him a friend and I had the opportunity to meet Fidel when my father passed away. It was also a real honour to meet his three sons and his brother President Raúl Castro during my recent visit to Cuba.*

On behalf of all Canadians, Sophie and I offer our deepest condolences to the family, friends and many, many supporters of Mr. Castro. We join the people of Cuba today in mourning the loss of this remarkable leader."

With those words Justin Trudeau branded himself an International Laughing Stock. He foisted that dubious prize upon the entire nation. He lavished praise on a brutal dictator who repressed and murdered his own people for half a century. In doing so Justin Trudeau proved I was not alone in thinking he had not visited Earth for a long time. In fact, I was in excellent company.

Michael Den Tandt said it best with the title of his *National Post* column.

"Earth to Trudeau — Fidel Castro was a brutal dictator, not a benevolent, grizzled uncle."

Den Tandt went on to write the following:

"Considering the furor in 2013 after Trudeau praised Communist China's 'basic dictatorship,' it is stupefying."

Stupefying indeed. Castro imprisoned, tortured and killed his political opponents. Families fled the island nation in droves, un-fazed by possible death on the open sea knowing certain death awaited them at home.

Canadians mocked Trudeau's love for Fidel Castro on Twitter using the hashtag #TrudeauEulogies. Here is a small sample of that mockery.

"Mr. Stalin's greatest achievement was his eradication of obesity in the Ukraine through innovative agricultural reforms. #TrudeauEulogies"

"With his innovative urban renewal program, Pol Pot bravely confronted the pressing challenge of overpopulation. #trudeaueulogies"

"We mourn the death of Vlad the Impaler, who spearheaded initiatives which touched the hearts of millions. #TrudeauEulogies #trudeaueulogy"

Amnesty International mustered the courage to say what Trudeau would not. Fidel Castro was a brutal dictator who monopolized print and broadcast media. He guaranteed the only opinions delivered to the Cuban people were those approved by Castro and his government.

Internet access is heavily censored in Cuba and until 2008 the simple ownership of a computer was banned. Can you even imagine that?

> *"The state of freedom of expression in Cuba, where activists continue to face arrest and harassment for speaking out against the government, is Fidel Castro's darkest legacy."*

Canadians expressed their disgust with Trudeau's praise of Fidel Castro. When Justin Trudeau's face appeared on the big screen at the 2016 Grey Cup game in Toronto they booed so loud Trudeau's voice is barely heard in the video posted on YouTube.

Hearing the crowd's disgust with him, Justin Trudeau could only wish for Castro's censorship powers over Canadians and their internet access.

One Twitter user wrote:

> *"Trudeau getting booed in the epicentre of Canada is my favourite thing ever"* #GreyCup

Canadian news commentators lamented that a Liberal Prime Minister could be so reviled this early in his first term. I don't know why. It makes perfect sense to me.

One final comment on Twitter caught my eye.

> *"If you voted for @JustinTrudeau you must be embarrassed. If you didn't vote for Justin you must be embarrassed for Canada. #TrudeauEulogies"*

Uh, yeah. Embarrassed for Canada is an understatement.

What Trudeau's Character Means For You

Researching and writing this book was truly an eye-opening experience. I intended to write something short and funny, something that mocked Justin Trudeau's many stupid statements. What I discovered was a pattern of deceit and hypocrisy so widespread it utterly blew my mind.

Justin Trudeau's pattern is crystal clear.

If you are willing to examine his words and actions for half an hour you will see it. Every minute you spend examining him beyond that only confirms your initial finding.

He says one thing and does the opposite. Every single time.

Every politician lies. We accept it. We shouldn't but we do. We accept it. Justin Trudeau takes that perception and blows it out of the water.

His sense of entitlement is limitless, as is his hypocrisy. I believed that before I started this book and yet my findings still surprised me.

What is so shocking is the depth and breadth of his contempt for the Canadian people. The citizens of Canada serve one purpose and one purpose only in Justin Trudeau's Canada. We are serfs paying tribute to an entitled king. That king believes Canada is his to use as he pleases. We *mere citizens* exist only pay the tab for his excess.

Canada is not important. Canadian citizens are not important.

The Justin Trudeau brand is important. It is the only important thing. It is everything.

A damning indictment? Absolutely. The evidence is clear and unassailable.

Regardless of your political leaning, I want you to ask yourself these two questions.

1. If Justin Trudeau cannot be trusted on his pet issue, feminism, can you believe him on any issue?

2. When Justin Trudeau proclaims himself defender of women then refuses to stop gender genocide through sex-selective abortion, can you trust him to defend women's rights?

This examination of Canada's 23rd Prime Minister revealed a man singularly focused on himself. His ego, arrogance and hubris drive his political agenda.

Our Prime Minister will say anything so long as it promotes the Justin Trudeau brand.

It's not about Canada and it's not about Canadians.

It's about Justin Trudeau.

Always.

A Fundamental Lack of Integrity

> **Integrity**: *moral soundness; firm adherence to a code of especially moral or artistic values; adherence to moral and ethical principles; soundness of moral character; honesty.*
>
> **Hypocrisy**: *a feigning to be what one is not or to believe what one does not; a pretense of having a virtuous character, moral or religious beliefs or principles, etc., that one does not really possess; a pretense of having some desirable or publicly approved attitude; a situation in which someone pretends to believe something that they do not really believe, or that is the opposite of what they do or say at another time.*

My examination of Justin Trudeau's words and actions reveal unbridled hypocrisy. It reveals a profound and fundamental lack of integrity.

Let's start with his mantra.

I am a Feminist

I have no issue with Justin Trudeau defining himself as a feminist. If he lived by that creed I would applaud him for it. He would be consistent.

Canada's celebrity feminist does not live true to that creed. He is not consistent. He pays lip service to it whenever a television camera is near.

Therein lies the problem. Trudeau's brand of feminism is hypocrisy personified. Justin Trudeau claims to defend women's rights. He does not. He refuses to condemn sex-selective abortion. He refuses to place any limits on abortion. He will not discuss ending the horrific practice. That cowardice condones and promotes gender genocide against unborn women.

Is that a defense of women's rights? No, of course not. Justin Trudeau's position on sex-selective abortion reveals his true colors: hypocrite and pro-abortion zealot.

> Marissa Semkiw: *"Yesterday you said you were happy with the status quo on abortion. But right now the status quo is that it's perfectly fine to abort a child because it's a girl. Do you have no qualms with that?"*

> Justin Trudeau: *"I will leave discussions like that between a woman and the health professionals that she encounters. I don't think the government should be in the business of legislating away people's rights. And that's why the Liberal Party is steadfast in this position."*

This is not leadership. This is Pablum.

Justin Trudeau abdicated his responsibility as a man, as a father, as a feminist and as a leader. Those little girls will never speak for themselves. They will never grow up to fawn over Prime Minister Selfie.

The duty to speak for those unborn baby girls rested with Justin Trudeau and he failed them. He committed unborn baby girls to death without so much as a whimper in their defence.

Reggie Littlejohn is the founder and president of Women's Rights without Frontiers. She condemned Justin Trudeau's hypocrisy.

> *"Aborting a baby just because she is a girl is the ultimate act of gender discrimination. It says that women are so worthless they don't deserve to be born. No one can say that they stand for women's rights without standing against the sex-selective abortion of future women. To say that you stand for women's rights and, at the same time, to support the sex-selective abortion of future women is hypocrisy."*

A true feminist would never advocate killing an unborn baby simply because that unborn baby is a girl. But that's just the thing, isn't it?

Justin Trudeau is not a true feminist. His feminism is an affectation. Trudeau's feminism is a veneer he puts on like a freshly laundered shirt before he shows it off in public.

That feminist affectation garners votes. That veneer appeals to a certain demographic. It blinds them to the stark reality Justin Trudeau supports sex-selective abortion, that he refuses to stop gender genocide against women.

Canada's celebrity feminist believes women are so worthless they do not even deserve to be born.

Ruth Ellen Brosseau

Justin Trudeau elbowed NDP MP Ruth Ellen Brosseau in the chest. The blow was significant. It forced Brosseau to leave the Parliamentary chamber to collect herself. A brave but visibly shaken Ruth Ellen Brosseau returned some time later.

Did Justin Trudeau, Canada's celebrity feminist, apologize to Ms. Brosseau?

No.

Well, yes. Sort of. But he took the coward's way out.

His only apology came in Parliament where television cameras dutifully recorded every stutter and stammer.

He never approached Ms. Brosseau away from television cameras. He never expressed regret for his hurtful actions to Ms. Brosseau directly.

Justin Trudeau's refusal to apologize to Ms. Brosseau revealed the yellow stripe of cowardice that runs down his back.

Those are not the actions of a feminist. They aren't even the actions of a man.

Heroic Defender of Barbarians

Justin Trudeau wants sensitivity for barbarians who carve up a woman's genitals. He wants their feelings protected. He wants 15 minutes of fame for his overblown sense of political correctness. Protecting women's genitals from being carved up by those barbarians? That doesn't even make the list of concerns for Canada's celebrity feminist.

A true feminist's primary concern is protecting women. A true feminist believes a woman's right to be safe from such atrocities is paramount. Not Justin Trudeau.

Spousal abuse, 'honour killings' and female genital mutilation are barbaric. Canada must condemn it, without exception. We cannot pander to the perpetrators of violence against women. Ever.

If that refusal hurts their little barbarian feelings, who cares?

Justin Trudeau cares.

His primary concern is for the tender feelings of degenerates who perform these heinous acts. Protecting women from female genital mutilation? Not so much.

Justin Trudeau's Catholic Faith

Justin Trudeau claims he is a faithful Catholic. Justin Trudeau opposes two fundamental tenets of Catholicism, abortion and same-sex marriage.

Justin Trudeau complains bitterly should anyone dare question his Catholic faith. His outrage is laughable. Justin Trudeau is a hypocrite on the issue he claims most important to him, his Catholic faith.

He will be far more hypocritical on those issues that mean far less.

That should terrify us all.

Opposes Mandatory Minimum Sentences for Child Molesters

Child molesters typically receive sentences of less than two years in prison. Canadian judges are loath to give appropriate prison terms to convicted sexual predators. That is unacceptable.

That is also why our previous Conservative government imposed mandatory minimum sentences for child sexual predators.

Justin Trudeau supports the repeal of mandatory minimum sentences for pedophiles. He values the liberty of convicted child molesters above the safety of Canadian children.

Our children have the right to be safe from degenerate sexual predators. Justin Trudeau will not reassure Canadian parents.

Ask yourself this question. Why does Prime Minister Justin Trudeau refuse to support mandatory minimum sentences for child sexual predators?

The Liberal Party is 100% Pro-Abortion

Justin Trudeau decreed the Liberal Party of Canada is pro-abortion. All Members of Parliament and all potential Liberal Party candidates must be pro-abortion. Even individual Liberal Party members must be pro-abortion. Trudeau will eject anyone who does not submit to his decree.

End of discussion for Justin Trudeau. Is it the end of the discussion for you?

Hypocrisy on Bill C-51

Prior to the 2015 election Justin Trudeau railed against Bill C-51, the Anti-Terrorism Act 2015. He then voted for the bill in Parliament.

Throughout the 2015 election campaign he vowed he would repeal the problematic portions of Bill C-51.

Prime Minister Justin Trudeau hasn't lifted a finger to do so. That refusal shows his true commitment to defending the rights and freedoms of Canadians. He does not have one.

Help for Canada's Middle Class

Justin Trudeau is a consummate actor. He panders to *mere citizens* for the most selfish of reasons: political power. His much-professed public love for Canada's middle class is another affectation. Like his feminism, Trudeau's profession of love for the middle class is an unnatural behaviour designed solely to impress.

Trudeau claims to defend the interests of Canada's middle class. He wants us to feel more confident about our prospects in his Brave New World yet his actions directly attack our livelihoods.

He will install a corrupt carbon tax scheme. He spent $5 billion outside Canada's borders in his first 100 days. He tripled down on his election promise of a $10 billion deficit in his first year. He promises massive deficits for the duration of his term as Prime Minister.

He has no plan to balance the budget. Ever. That does not help Canada's middle class. It buries us under a mountain of debt with a carbon tax on top.

Immigration

Justin Trudeau's plan to bring 25,000 Syrian refugees into Canada exposed his love of photo ops and selfies. He completely ignored the needs of communities forced to deal with his personal agenda.

Trudeau refused to put resources in place to deal with a massive influx of refugees. Most young Syrian refugees do not understand Canadian culture. They do not speak our official languages. There are no language classes for them.

Canadian children, as Fredericton High School proved, pay the price. Our children must fend for themselves. Canadian children suffer physical abuse and sexual harassment at the hands of young Syrian men.

Justin Trudeau, his required photo ops and selfies over, is MIA.

Good Government and Massive Deficits

> *"I believe in fiscal responsibility and I quite frankly I think Liberals ... are more motivated to therefore to do them well, do them responsibly, not going to massive deficits the way certain other governments who have been less motivated to deliver good government have."*

Justin Trudeau wants us to believe he thinks good government and massive deficits are polar opposites. He wants us to believe a government, not his of course, running massive deficits is one less motivated to deliver good government.

Then Trudeau delivered a $34 billion deficit for fiscal 2016/17. He plans to run a $120 billion deficit for the rest of his term.

This is Justin Trudeau's idea of good government?

Not once during the election did the mainstream media scrutinize Trudeau. They did not add up his massive spending promises. They did not examine his carbon tax designed to pander to the United Nations and environmental extremists.

It's also a plan guaranteed to rob his much-loved middle class of another $2,500 each year.

Your grandchildren will pay the freight for Justin Trudeau's excesses today. That's the Liberal way.

Who cares how much we spend? Paying it back is someone else's problem.

Broken Promise on Restoring Canada Post Home Delivery

Trudeau committed to restoring Canada Post home delivery to almost a million Canadians. Once elected, that promise morphed into a commitment to undertake a new review of Canada Post. After that review we're left with a potential for restoring home delivery.

Even that potential restoration would be one or two days a week, if at all.

Constitutionally Illiterate

> *"The segregation of French and English in schools [in New Brunswick] is something to be looked at seriously. It is dividing people and affixing labels to people."*

Pierre Elliott Trudeau brought us the Canadian Charter of Rights and Freedoms. Justin Trudeau is so constitutionally illiterate he had no idea Francophones are guaranteed separate schools under our constitution.

Only after he was reprimanded in public by his own party did Trudeau comprehend the magnitude of his ignorance.

Growing the Economy from the Heart Outwards

Everything Justin Trudeau learned about growing an economy he learned at the feet of his father.

Justin Trudeau's spending obsession thru 2019, like his father's spending obsession in the 1970s and 1980s, will bury Canadians with massive debt. Trudeau the Elder increased Canada's national debt by a mind-numbing 787%. Nobody else in our history even comes close.

Until now. His son, Prime Minister Justin Trudeau, plans do it again.

Justin's Love of Dictatorships and Dictators

Pierre Trudeau passed his love of communist dictators on to his son. Justin Trudeau, to our national horror, embraced that love with all his heart. His glowing tribute to Fidel Castro proved he did not learn from his *I admire China's basic dictatorship* debacle. It also turned him into an international laughingstock.

A stadium filled with irate Canadians rewarded his delusion by booing him non-stop at the 2016 Grey Cup. How appropriate, given Justin Trudeau's admiration for people who don't think about politics.

Trudeau the Younger wants no part of an informed and politically active citizenry. He admires uninformed citizens disconnected from the political process. He admires people who don't care what he does and don't pay attention to it either.

Trudeau's attitude is sickening but not unexpected. He loves dictators. It stands to reason he loves the power they wield over their citizens as well. That is scary, given his admiration for China's basic dictatorship and Cuban dictator Fidel Castro. He longs for a dictator's unfettered power and control over a nation.

When our Prime Minister does not value accountability we *mere citizens* are right to worry. Trudeau's love for dictatorships sends a signal flare high in the sky, a warning to us all. We must pay attention to that warning, regardless of our political leaning.

Justin Trudeau's admiration for dictatorships also explains his position on electoral reform.

Electoral Reform Only if it Benefits Liberal Party

Justin Trudeau wants electoral reform so long as it benefits the Liberal Party of Canada. That's also why he refuses to hold a referendum on electoral reform. The opinions of *mere citizens* do not concern him.

We exist only to pay the bills for his extravagance.

The Liberal Party isn't happy with forming government 70% of the last 57 years. They want 100%. If Justin Trudeau imposes preferential balloting upon us that's precisely what we'll get.

Trudeau's Promise of Open Government and Transparency

> *"We have also committed to set a higher bar for openness and transparency in government. It is time to shine more light on government to ensure it remains focused on the people it serves. Government and its information should be open by default."*

This promise lasted all the way to the election results. Three seconds later Trudeau's promise of government openness and transparency vanished.

He refused to prosecute First Nations bands for non-compliance with the First Nations Financial Transparency Act. This signaled how a Justin Trudeau government would deal with transparency for the duration of his term.

It wouldn't.

Gun Control

Justin Trudeau is both for and against the gun registry. It depends on which official language he speaks and whether he stands on Quebec soil or not. Speaking in French on Quebec soil the long gun registry is a great idea. Speaking in English anywhere else it's a bad plan and he will not to bring it back.

Which is the truth? That is impossible to know, for sure, but there are warning signs.

Liberal Senator Celine Hervieux-Payette wanted to ban guns. She would graciously allow us to keep those she deemed acceptable for hunting.

Would she introduce her Senate bill without the express permission and support of her Liberal Party leader?

Not likely. The smart money says Justin Trudeau wants to ban guns. The smart money says his words inside Quebec are his true feelings. This brings me to my next point. Justin Trudeau's statements inside Quebec and their conflict with his statements to the rest of Canada.

Quebec First, Foremost and Always

> *"We have 24 senators in Quebec and there are only six*
> *for Alberta and British Columbia. That benefits us. It*
> *is an advantage for Quebec."*

Justin Trudeau's primary allegiance is, first, foremost and always, to Quebec. When push comes to shove it's Quebec's interests he protects, not Canada's. The rest of Canada exists to pay Quebec's bills.

Justin Trudeau denigrates the west while he asserts Quebec's superiority in all things. He does this repeatedly in French, inside Quebec.

> *"Certainly when we look at the great prime ministers of*
> *the 20th century, those that really stood the test of time,*
> *they were MPs from Quebec… This country – Canada –*
> *it belongs to us."*

That is not the leadership Canadians deserve. It is, however, the leadership they voted for in 2015. I pray our nation survives that disastrous decision but early indicators are not good.

Will Not Condemn Terrorism or Genocide

Citizenship is a privilege. Committing an act of terrorism violates that privilege. It is proper to revoke Canadian citizenship from convicted terrorists. They proved they do not deserve the privilege of being a Canadian. It is reprehensible for a Canadian Prime Minister to say otherwise.

Justin Trudeau says terrorists are just misunderstood. He insists we must empathize with them so terrorists will love us more and kill us less.

Justin Trudeau visits Islamic mosques regularly. He visited the Brossard Islamic Community Centre, home of radical Imam Foudil Selmoune.

Selmoune wants Sharia law implemented in Canada so he can cut off the hands of people *who have money and who steal*. Selmoune's mosque gave money to a terrorist organization. Regular attendees of his mosque are currently in prison, convicted of terrorist crimes.

This is Justin Trudeau's desired multicultural fabric? He would subject all Canadians to Sharia law and kill all opposed to Islam?

Awesome.

Small Businesses are Frauds and Tax Evaders

Justin Trudeau believes most small businesses are tax shelters for the rich. He cannot fathom Canada's small businesses create 70% of all jobs in Canada, employing millions. Nope, nothing but tax havens for the wealthy, he says.

Hypocrisy on the Temporary Foreign Worker program

Justin Trudeau railed against the Temporary Foreign Worker program in public, yet privately hired a nanny through that same program.

Leadership

Justin Trudeau has a history of swearing in Parliament. After every vulgar outburst his response is the same.

> *"I lost my temper and used language that was most decidedly unparliamentary and for that I unreservedly apologize."*

He apologizes but he never learns from his childish outbursts. He never modifies his behavior to act like a leader.

He cursed at a charity fundraising event for cancer. Afterward Trudeau hid behind his wife's skirts. Then he blamed Stephen Harper to avoid taking responsibility for his actions.

His primary concern is always the same. Perpetuating the Trudeau brand at the expense of the *mere citizens* of Canada.

We're just here to pay for his whims and his sense of entitlement.

Culture of Entitlement

Justin Trudeau's first Prime Ministerial act was the calling card of his entitlement. He signed an order for two nannies for his children. He forced the *mere citizens* of Canada to pay them. So much for his claim that *wealthy families like mine* don't need child care benefits.

If you believe nothing else I've written you cannot wash away the stain of Justin Trudeau's sense of entitlement. Even the most hard core Trudeau acolyte must admit that.

The Media Will Not Hold Him Accountable

Justin Trudeau is first, foremost and always a Quebecer. The remainder of Canada is a distant… who can even say how far down his list of priorities.

o   Justin Trudeau is a hypocrite on feminism.
o   Justin Trudeau is a hypocrite on abortion.
o   Justin Trudeau is a hypocrite on defending women's rights.
o   Justin Trudeau is a hypocrite on his own religious beliefs.
o   Justin Trudeau is a hypocrite on Bill C-51.
o   Justin Trudeau is a hypocrite on Canada Post home delivery.
o   Justin Trudeau is a hypocrite on gun control.
o   Justin Trudeau is a hypocrite on the Temporary Foreign Worker Program.
o   Justin Trudeau has an unbridled sense of entitlement.
o   Justin Trudeau has an unfettered love of dictators and dictatorships, and all things Islam.

The list goes on and on and on. Canada's national media fawns over our Prime Minister and refuses to hold him accountable.

What about you?

Do you have an issue with Justin Trudeau's massive integrity deficit?

Will you hold him accountable for his hypocrisy?

Remember those answers when you cast your ballot in 2019.

One Last Thing!

First, thank you for reading this book!

If you enjoyed this book (and even if you did not) I would be grateful if you would post an honest review on Amazon and/or Goodreads. Every review helps this book find more readers, the lifeblood of any author.

http://ChristopherDiArmani.net/Review-Trudeau-Book-on-Amazon
http://ChristopherDiArmani.net/Review-Trudeau-Book-on-Goodreads

Your support in the form of an honest review really does make a difference. I also read every review as part of my efforts to can make my books even better.

I would also be grateful if you shared this book on your social media accounts.

If, for some reason, you did not like this book or didn't get what you expected out of it please tell me directly so I can use your constructive criticism to update the book to meet your expectations. You can contact me here:

http://ChristopherDiArmani.net/Contact

Thank you so much for your support, feedback and your honest reviews.

Sincerely,

Christopher di Armani
Author Extraordinare
http://ChristopherDiArmani.net/Books

About Christopher di Armani

"Author Extraordinaire"

The hardest writing for any author, I suspect, is writing about themselves. It sure is for me.

While I can write the most personal quirks, the most embarrassing situations and tell the truth for any character in my fiction, writing about myself is, well, uncomfortable.

I'm not one for the spotlight. I like the shadows. I'm most comfortable there. Most writers are.

Writing is my passion and I'm my happiest when I'm pounding out a story. If it's 3am and I'm still at the keyboard you are right to be scared.

Anything can show up on the page at that hour.

Like many writers I am an avid reader. My earliest memories are of Zane Grey westerns. I devoured them like candy.

His strong male characters would, no matter their personal flaws, do the right thing when it mattered most. That is what drew me to his books.

I imagine I learned a lot of my own moral code from the characters Zane Grey created.

Like many writers I am also an introvert. Do not allow the protestations of past co-workers convince you otherwise. They see what I want them to see - the social face that allows me to function out in the world. Every writer has one.

It's how we survive until we make our way back to the safety and security of our writing room.

I am a good writer.

That's not arrogance speaking. That's a fact substantiated by the money folks pay me to write. Bad writers don't get paid.

I didn't start off a good writer though.

My first novel, written when I was 16, is proof of that. It's about teenage gangs in high school, about bad choices and worse friends. I wrote it as an assignment for English class. My teacher took pity on me and commended me for its length and ambition with a C Plus. Notice he did not say *talent*.

The book is horrible. Really. I stumbled across it a few years ago and attempted to read it. By the end of the first page I wanted to vomit. It's trash.

I accept that.

I started writing young and wrote anything that struck my fancy. Some of it was published, most wasn't. I wrote letters to the editor, newspaper articles, short stories, poetry, novellas, books, screenplays and short films.

Major newspapers, both print and digital, published me as time went on. Then I edited a national magazine for a firearms advocacy group for two years. That's where I learned first-hand just how hard we writers make things for our editors.

During my tenure as magazine editor I learned how to edit *anything* into readable form. Why? I had to meet deadline. That's a lesson that serves me well to this day.

I'm also a huge horror movie fan. I love vampires (*not the ones that sparkle*), werewolves and scary guys like Hannibal Lecter.

My interests vary widely as do my forms and genres of writing. I love writing current events commentary. That love has turned into numerous book projects, including a book on the RCMP's ongoing issues as well as a book on Canada's 23rd Prime Minister, Justin Trudeau.

I've written a vampire movie, series of two serial killer movies in a series and I'm in the process of turning all three scripts into books. I just finished the first draft of the novel based on the vampire script and so far so good. When I finish that I'll turn the two serial killer movies into novels and add the third and final installment to that series. Along the way I'm sure I will write other odd things, too.

Like most writers I have more ideas than I have time to write. That's the beauty of the creative mind, isn't it?

I also love art but cannot draw to save my life. Hold a gun to my head and say "draw or die" and I'll make my peace with God while awaiting your bullet. The good Lord gave me many talents. Drawing is not one of them. That's why I love Poser, a 3D image creation and animation program. It allows me to fulfill my artistic desires despite my complete lack of artistic ability.

As a writer I love Poser. I use it to create character reference images for my stories. Like most writers I have a concrete vision of who my characters are, what they look like, what they wear, how they hold themselves, etc.

Poser allows me to create these character reference images quickly and easily. I pin them to the wall and stare at them when I need inspiration and I cannot count the times these reference images have helped me when I was stuck.

If you've managed to get to the end of this wandering diatribe I both thank you for your patience and commend you for your perseverance. There's nothing worse than reading about someone droning on about themselves!

Since you're still here, however, I'd love to keep you updated about what I'm writing next. Just visit the link below to join my mailing list.

http://ChristopherDiArmani.net/Trudeau-Reader-Subscription-Form/

Until our paths cross again…

Christopher di Armani
Author Extraordinaire
http://ChristopherDiArmani.net/Books

Books by Christopher di Armani

The Simple 3-Step Secret to Slaughter Writer's Block And Vanquish it Forever

There is no more perfect Hell than one where I cannot write.

You know that terror, too, don't you? That sense your last remaining creative spark abandoned you some time back. It's sickening.

Allow me to teach you how to extricate yourself, once and for all, from that perfect Hell and never return.

This simple 3-step solution will work for you provided you follow these instructions to the letter. Guaranteed.

******

Christopher di Armani delivers a message every writer should hear with wit and sarcasm. This humorous look at writer's block is an easy read with proven results.

http://ChristopherDiArmani.net/Writers-Block-Book

TOP SECRET - Inspiration, Motivation and Encouragement - 701 Essential Quotes for Writers

This compilation of 701 quotes delivers inspiration, motivation and encouragement on 39 aspects of writing and the writing life.

You will discover quotes to make you laugh and quotes to make you cry. Some are familiar, like old friends. Others you will meet for the first time. All have a common theme: The Writing Life.

Writers may sit alone in our writing rooms but we experience the same emotions. We share our wit and wisdom. We learn from each other.

This book is a resource. Use it when you need inspiration or encouragement. Use it when you need motivation to write.

Take time to reflect on the wisdom in these pages. There is much to learn from the great writers of our day and of days gone by. The words of these past masters will keep you in times of darkness. They will light your way. They will pick you up when you are down. They will ground you when your ego gets too large.

Above all they will remind you that writers, all writers, are part of our fragile humanity.

We must, above all, be kind to each other.

http://ChristopherDiArmani.net /Top-Secret-Quotes

Justin Trudeau - 47 Character-Revealing Quotes from Canada's 23rd Prime Minister and What They Mean for You

On October 19, 2015 Canadians elected their 23rd Prime Minister based on good looks, nice hair and a famous name. They voted for style over substance.

Our 23rd Prime Minister's entire leadership experience consisted of teaching snowboarding lessons and high school drama. His management experience consisted of administering his trust fund and his ego.

Not a single thought was given to what he stood for, what his party stood for, or what he would actually do once elected to the highest office in the land.

That bothered me. That bothered me so much I began to research his much-publicized missteps and that in turn revealed a disturbing pattern within Trudeau's numerous faux pas.

That pattern is the focus of this book.

http://ChristopherDiArmani.net/Justin-Trudeau-Book-1

**Are you interested in some amazingly
beautiful yet haunting music?**

Check out

London Grammar

http://www.LondonGrammar.com/

I discovered London Grammar through a fellow writer just as I began editing this book. He listed their hit "Strong" as the first title in the soundtrack for the movie of his book. I fell in love with it. Never did get to the rest of his soundtrack. London Grammar's YouTube channel became my editing backdrop through a dozen or more editing passes.

London Grammar's music and vocals are beautiful. Haunting. Their video for "Strong" is incredible. Watch it. You will be blown away by its visuals, just as I was.

Coming Soon

Maryam Monsef: The Meteoric Rise and Fall of Canada's Most Famous Refugee

Justin Trudeau's commitment to cabinet gender parity guaranteed two things. First and most obvious, an equal number of men and women would sit in cabinet. Second, some of those cabinet members would not possess the skills required to do the job.

His January 2017 cabinet shuffle proved this inevitable and undeniable truth.

Justin Trudeau ranks gender and minority status above skill and talent. His wilful blindness does not permit him to see his rising political stars are nothing more than shiny objects in the night sky. Dazzling and captivating in the moment but without the power to effect the real change he promised on the campaign trail.

Maryam Monsef's bubbly persona could not hide the painful truth. She was in over her head, a fact plainly obvious to everyone except Justin Trudeau.

Her entire political experience consisted of one failed mayoral election campaign and one successful federal election campaign.

She's a good campaigner. That does not automatically translate into the skill required of a cabinet minister.

This book traces Maryam Monsef's roots in Iran and Afghanistan to Canada and her entry into politics. It tracks her meteoric rise to political prominence. It tracks the brilliant light of her political career as it streaked across the night sky, burning up all her political promise.

RCMP Thugs, Thieves and Liars: The Appalling Lack of Accountability in Canada's National Police Force

The RCMP's deep, plentiful and systemic problems lend to much spilled ink by writers like me.

They make the RCMP an easy target for commentators who, for one reason or another, dislike one or more of the following: cops, the RCMP, thugs in uniform, thieves in uniform, serial sexual abusers, bullies and an internal system of discipline that is a rude joke.

Me, I don't dislike cops in general. In fact I cannot think of a single interaction with a uniformed RCMP member that has left a bad feeling in my mouth.

The RCMP's lack of accountability, however, is another story entirely.

Chapter & Section Citations

Justin Trudeau's Leadership

Sometimes I Say Stupid Things

o   Raj, Althia. "Justin Trudeau Says Stephen Harper's Ego Is Driving Combat Mission In Iraq." *The Huffington Post*, Oct 20, 2014, huffingtonpost.ca/2014/10/20/justin-trudeau-iraq-harper-ego_n_6018632.html. Accessed Nov 1, 2016.

World Stupidity Awards

o   leif. "bush wins big at world stupidity awards." Daily Kos, Jul 24, 2004, dailykos.com/story/2004/07/24/39924/-bush-wins-big-at-world-stupidity-awards. Accessed Nov 1, 2016.

Someone Will Tell Me if Something Important Happens

o   Palmer, Randall. "Canada's new Trudeau channels Kennedy and Obama, but can he win?" *Reuters*, Apr 10, 2013, reuters.com/article/us-trudeau-idUSBRE9390SJ20130410. Accessed Nov 28, 2016.

Our Childish Prime Minister

o   globalnewsdotca. "Canadian politician Trudeau yells swear word during debate." *Global News*, Dec 15, 2011, youtube.com/watch?v=TZ2FmGOU4tE. Accessed Nov 2, 2016.
o   National Post Staff. "Uproar as Justin Trudeau hurls four-letter obscenity at Peter Kent in House of Commons." *Global News*, Dec 14, 2011, youtube.com/watch?v=TZ2FmGOU4tE. Accessed Nov 2, 2016.
o   National Post Staff. "Uproar as Justin Trudeau hurls four-letter obscenity at Peter Kent in House of Commons." *National Post*, Dec 14, 2011, news.nationalpost.com/news/canada/justin-trudeau-allegedly-calls-peter-kent-a-piece-of-s-in-commons. Accessed Nov 2, 2016.
o   Ivison, John. "Justin Trudeau's 'shiddle-diddle' moment with Peter Kent ignites final QP of 2011." *National Post*, Dec 14,

2011, news.nationalpost.com/full-comment/john-ivison-justin-trudeaus-shiddle-diddle-moment-reminds-us-why-question-period-is-worth-watching. Accessed Nov 2, 2016.

o Russell, Andrew. "'I saw him stick his tongue out': Trudeau accused of 'childish behaviour' in House of Commons." *National Post*, May 6, 2016, globalnews.ca/news/2684793/i-saw-him-stick-his-tongue-out-trudeau-accused-of-childish-behaviour-in-house-of-commons/?sf25789297=1. Accessed Nov 2, 2016.

o Fitzpatrick, Meagan. "Justin Trudeau apologizes for swearing at Kent." *CBC News*, Dec 14, 2011, cbc.ca/news/politics/justin-trudeau-apologizes-for-swearing-at-kent-1.995992. Accessed Nov 28, 2016.

o Various Speakers, "Department of the Environment Questions." Hansard - 124, May 5, 2012, http://www.parl.gc.ca/parliamentarians/en/publicationsearch?View=D&Item=&ParlSes=41-1&oob=&Topic=&Per=&Prov=&Cauc=&Text=Megan%20Leslie%20durban&RPP=15&order=&targetLang=&SBS=0&MRR=150000&Page=1&PubType=37. Accessed Nov 2, 2016.

Trudeau's Charity Fundraiser F-Bomb

o Trudeau, Justin. "Trudeau Fighting Words " *YouTube.com*, Mar 29, 2014, youtube.com/watch?time_continue=109&v=UuHDCmanRW0. Accessed Nov 1, 2016.

o McGregor, Glen. "Justin Trudeau drops f-bomb at charity event." *Ottawa Citizen*, Mar 30, 2014, ottawacitizen.com/uncategorized/justin-trudeau-drops-f-bomb-at-charity-event. Accessed Nov 1, 2016.

o CTVNews.ca Staff. "Justin Trudeau's charity event f-bomb shows 'lack of judgment': PMO." *CTV News*, Mar 30, 2014, ctvnews.ca/politics/justin-trudeau-s-charity-event-f-bomb-shows-lack-of-judgment-pmo-1.1753214. Accessed Nov 1, 2016.

o Hume, Jessica. "Justin Trudeau sorry for F-bomb at charity boxing event." *London Free Press*, Mar 31, 2014, lfpress.com/2014/03/31/justin-trudeau-drops-f-bomb-at-charity-boxing-event. Accessed Nov 1, 2016.

Eve Adams a Liberal Candidate? Over My Dead Body!

o Clark, Campbell. "Eve Adams's failed nomination bid casts doubts on Trudeau's judgment." *Globe and Mail*, Jul 27, 2015, theglobeandmail.com/news/politics/eve-adamss-failed-nomination-bid-casts-doubts-on-trudeaus-judgment/article25725975/. Accessed Nov 7, 2016.
o Berthiaume, Lee. "Justin Trudeau champions Liberals' open nominations amid allegations party blocked certain candidates." *National Post*, Dec 11, 2014, news.nationalpost.com/news/canada/canadian-politics/justin-trudeau-champions-liberals-open-nominations-amid-allegations-party-blocked-certain-candidates. Accessed Nov 7, 2016.

Constitution / Legal Rights

Whose Father Created the Charter of Rights and Freedoms?

o LeBlanc, Daniel. "Justin Trudeau apologizes over French school comment." *Globe and Mail*, May 07, 2007, theglobeandmail.com/news/national/justin-trudeau-apologizes-over-french-school-comment/article1075760/. Accessed Nov 21,2016.

It's Alberta's Fault and "we Quebecers, Canada belongs to us."

o Lagacé, Patrick. "Justin Trudeau Interview." Émission Les Francs-Tireurs, Nov 24, 2010, lesfrancstireurs.telequebec.tv/occurrence.aspx?id=134. Accessed Dec 1, 2016.
o Wherry, Aaron. "'Because it's Albertans who control our community and socio-democratic agenda'." *MacLean's Magazine*, Nov 22, 2012, www.macleans.ca/politics/ottawa/because-its-albertans-who-control-our-community-and-socio-democratic-agenda, Accessed Dec 12, 2016
o CBC News. "Trudeau campaign forced to address 2010 comments on Alberta." CBC News, Nov 22, 2012, cbc.ca/news/politics/trudeau-campaign-forced-to-address-2010-comments-on-alberta-1.1241750. Accessed Nov 18, 2016.

- o Department of Finance Canada. "Federal Support to Provinces and Territories." *Department of Finance Canada*, Oct 24, 2016, www.fin.gc.ca/fedprov/mtp-eng.asp. Accessed Nov 12, 2016.
- o Canadian Press, The. "Justin Trudeau's anti-Alberta remarks aren't going over well in Quebec either." National Post, Nov 24, 2012, news.nationalpost.com/news/canada/justin-trudeaus-anti-alberta-remarks-arent-going-over-well-in-quebec-either. Accessed Nov 21, 2016.

Justin Trudeau Would Help Quebec Separate

- o Craine, Patrick. "Justin Trudeau will back Quebec separatists if Harper restricts abortion?" LivesiteNwes.com, Feb 14, 2012, www.lifesitenews.com/news/justin-trudeau-will-back-quebec-separatists-if-harper-restricts-abortion. Accessed Nov 12, 2016
- o Trudeau, Pierre Elliott. *Transcript of a speech given by the Right Honourable Pierre Elliott Trudeau at the Paul Sauvé Arena in Montreal on May 14, 1980.* [Ottawa]: Office of the Prime Minister, 1980. 15 p.

Quebec Deserves More

- o Murphy, Jessica. "Trudeau defends Senate comments ." *Toronto Sun*, May 27, 2013, torontosun.com/2013/05/27/trudeau-defends-senate-comments. Accessed Nov 22, 2016
- o MacKinnon, Leslie. "Harper not in question period to address Senate scandal." CBC News, May 27, 2013, www.cbc.ca/news/politics/harper-not-in-question-period-to-address-senate-scandal-1.1312827. Accessed Nov 15, 2016

Justin Trudeau's Hypocrisy on "Open Government"

- o Murphy, Rex. "Electoral Reform." *The National*, May 19, 2016, www.cbc.ca/player/play/689060931669/. Accessed November 12, 2016.
- o Grenier, Éric. "Change to preferential ballot would benefit Liberals." *CBC News*, Nov 26, 2015, www.cbc.ca/news/politics/grenier-preferential-ballot-1.3332566., Accessed Nov 26, 2015.
- o NDP Party Platform. "NDP and Fair Vote Canada stand up for electoral reform." *NDP*, Dec 15th, 2014, www.ndp.ca/news/ndp-

and-fair-vote-canada-stand-electoral-reform. Accessed Nov 15th, 2016.

o Bryden, Joan. "Justin Trudeau denies electoral reform favours Liberal party." *Global News*, Dec 17, 2015, globalnews.ca/news/2406513/justin-trudeau-denies-electoral-reform-favours-liberal-party/. Accessed Nov 17, 2016.

o Every Voter Counts Alliance, "Every Voter Counts FAQ." *Every Voter Counts Alliance*, Unknown, www.everyvotercounts.ca/faq2/. Accessed Nov 14, 2016.

o Ryckewaert, Laura. "Most want referendum on electoral reform, new poll suggests, question dominates initial House committee, feds deke and dodge." *The Hill Times*, Jul 11, 2016, www.hilltimes.com/2016/07/11/referendum-question-dominates-initial-electoral-reform-committee-work/73344, Accessed Nov 12, 2016.

o Bozinoff, Dr. Lorne. "Two Thirds See Need For Referendum On Electoral Reform." *Forum Research Inc.*, Jul 11, 2016, poll.forumresearch.com/post/2547/two-thirds-see-need-for-referendum-on-electoral-reform/. Accessed Nov 9, 2016.

o Conservative Party of Canada. "Protect Your Vote." Conservative Party of Canada, Unknown, www.conservative.ca/cpc/protect-your-vote/. Accessed Nov 16, 2016.

o Halevi, Jonathan D. "Trudeau Implies: Reformed Electoral System Will Give Advantage To The Liberals." *Christian Defence League*, Apr 22, 2016, christiandefenceleague.com/pdf/Reformed%20Electoral.pdf. Accessed Nov 2, 2016.

Of Open Nominations, Winners and... Not Winners?

o CBC News. "Barj Dhahan says Liberals pressured him to withdraw from Vancouver South race." *CBC News*, Dec 23, 2014, www.cbc.ca/news/canada/british-columbia/barj-dhahan-says-liberals-pressured-him-to-withdraw-from-vancouver-south-race-1.2882010. Accessed Nov 5, 2016.

o CBC News. "Justin Trudeau goes one-on-one with CBC host Andrew Chang." *CBC News*, Dec 18, 2014, www.cbc.ca/news/canada/british-columbia/justin-trudeau-goes-one-on-one-with-cbc-host-andrew-chang-1.2878612. Accessed Nov 5, 2016.

Would-Be Liberal Candidate Christine Innes Sues Justin Trudeau

o   Bryden, Joan. "Justin Trudeau says he's committed to open nominations — despite banning a candidate over bullying claims." *The Canadian Press*, Mar 19, 2014, news.nationalpost.com/news/canada/canadian-politics/justin-trudeau-says-hes-committed-to-open-nominations-despite-banning-a-candidate-over-bullying-claims. Accessed Nov 1, 2016.

o   CBC News. "Thwarted Liberal candidate Christine Innes sues Justin Trudeau for defamation." *CBC News*, Apr 14, 2014, www.cbc.ca/news/politics/thwarted-liberal-candidate-christine-innes-sues-justin-trudeau-for-defamation-1.2610158. Accessed Nov 1, 2016.

o   CBC News. "Thwarted Liberal candidate Christine Innes sues Justin Trudeau for defamation." *CBC News*, Mar 13, 2014, www.cbc.ca/news/politics/read-christine-innes-letter-to-supporters-here-1.2571817. Accessed Nov 1, 2016.

Zach Paikin's Integrity (and Justin's Lack of it)

o   CBC News. "Zach Paikin criticizes Justin Trudeau as he ends Liberal nomination bid." *CBC News*, Mar 17, 2014, www.cbc.ca/news/politics/zach-paikin-criticizes-justin-trudeau-as-he-ends-liberal-nomination-bid-1.2576147. Accessed Nov 1, 2016

Rob Ford Need Not Apply

o   Stroumboulopoulos, George. "George Stroumboulopoulos Tonight." *CBC*, Apr 1, 2014, www.cbc.ca/strombo/videos/web-exclusive/justin-trudeau-liberal-candidates-rob-ford. Accessed Aug 25, 2016.

o   Visser, Josh. "Justin Trudeau makes another swear, rules out Rob Ford running for Liberals in chummy CBC interview." *National Post*, Apr 2, 2014, news.nationalpost.com/news/canada/canadian-politics/justin-trudeau-makes-another-swear-rules-out-rob-ford-running-for-liberals-in-chummy-cbc-interview. Accessed Nov 5, 2016.

Referendums are pretty good way of not getting electoral reform

- o Bozinoff, Dr. Lorne. "Two Thirds See Need For Referendum On Electoral Reform." *Forum Research Inc.*, Jul 11, 2016, poll.forumresearch.com/post/2547/two-thirds-see-need-for-referendum-on-electoral-reform/. Accessed Nov 9, 2016.
- o Murphy, Rex. "Electoral Reform." *The National*, May 19, 2016, www.cbc.ca/player/play/689060931669/. Accessed November 12, 2016.
- o Ambrose, Rona. "Referendum the only legitimate way to reform the electoral system." *Conservative Party of Canada*, Dec 28, 2015, www.conservative.ca/referendum-the-only-legitimate-way-to-reform-the-electoral-system-ambrose/. Accessed Nov 12, 2016.

Senators Removed from Liberal Caucus

- o CTV News. The quote *"I am the leader of the Liberal Party. I decide who is in the Senate."* (January 31, 2014) is scrubbed from CTV's site. Quote is cited on https://voat.co/v/news/1598037 with CTV attribution.
- o CBC News. "Justin Trudeau statement: 'Senate is broken, and needs to be fixed'." *CBC News*, Jan 29, 2014, www.cbc.ca/news/politics/justin-trudeau-statement-senate-is-broken-and-needs-to-be-fixed-1.2515374. Accessed Nov 1, 2016
- o Cudmore, James. "Justin Trudeau removes senators from Liberal caucus." *CBC News*, Jan 29, 2014, www.cbc.ca/news/politics/justin-trudeau-removes-senators-from-liberal-caucus-1.2515273. Accessed Nov 1, 2016
- o The Canadian Press. "The road taken by Justin Trudeau to his Senate reform decision." *CBC News*, Jan 30, 2014, www.cbc.ca/news/politics/the-road-taken-by-justin-trudeau-to-his-senate-reform-decision-1.2516793. Accessed Nov 4, 2016.
- o Goldy, Faith, "Justin Trudeau Runs From Sun News hard Questions", 2014, Sun News Network, http://video.news.canoe.ca/video/hub/news/2525479625001/justin-trudeau-runs-from-sun-news-hard-questions/3127087241001. Accessed Nov 1, 2016.

Trudeau's Culture of Entitlement Benefits Politicians

- Blatchford, Andy. "Japan's prime minister puts heat on Trudeau over TPP, South China Sea." *Toronto Star*, May 24, 2016, www.thestar.com/news/canada/2016/05/24/justin-trudeau-to-take-day-off-during-japan-trip-to-celebrate-wedding-anniversary.html. Accessed Dec 12, 2016.
- Fekete, Jason. "MPs, senators get pay hike as Canadians struggle with stagnant wages, rising unemployment." *Ottawa Citizen*, Mar 31, 2016, news.nationalpost.com/news/canada/mps-senators-get-pay-hike-as-canadians-struggle-with-stagnant-wages-rising-unemployment. Accessed Dec 3, 2016.
- Workopolis, "So, how much are we earning? The average Canadian salaries by industry and region." *Workopolis*, Nov 30, 2016, careers.workopolis.com/advice/how-much-money-are-we-earning-the-average-canadian-wages-right-now/. Accessed Dec 4, 2016.
- Hopkins, Andrea and Ljunggren, David. "Trudeau says $30B budget deficit not hard limit." *Reuters*, May 19, 2016, www.torontosun.com/2016/05/19/trudeau-says-30b-budget-deficit-not-hard-limit. Accessed Dec 5, 2016.
- Beardsley, Keith. "Trudeau's Spending Priorities Send Too Many Tax Dollars Overseas." *Huffington Post*, Feb 16, 2016, www.huffingtonpost.ca/keith-beardsley/trudeau-deficit_b_9226722.html. Accessed Dec 12, 2016.

Taxpayer-Funded Nannies

- Hall, Chris. "Trudeau children's nannies being paid for by taxpayers." *CBC News*, Nov 30, 2015, www.cbc.ca/news/politics/justin-trudeau-nannies-taxpayers-1.3344533. Accessed Nov 4, 2016.
- Levant, Ezra. "Pay for your own nannies, Justin!" *TheRebel Media*, Unknown, www.therebel.media/payforyourownnanny, Accessed Nov 3, 2016.
- The Canadian Press. "Conservatives and NDP blast Trudeau's wife for wanting extra staff to help with her official duties." National Post, May 13, 2016, news.nationalpost.com/news/canada/canadian-politics/conservatives-and-ndp-blast-trudeaus-wife-for-wanting-extra-staff-to-help-with-her-official-duties. Accessed Nov 12, 2016.

- Levant, Ezra. "Twitter Post." *Twitter.com*, Sep 30, 2016, twitter.com/ezralevant/status/778364277560311808. Accessed Nov 12, 2016.
- Kenney, Jason. "Twitter Post." *Twitter.com*, May 12, 2016, twitter.com/jkenney/status/730922805181616130. Accessed Nov 12, 2016.

I Have Tremendous Confidence...

- Trudeau, Justin. "Justin Trudeau CNN interview in Davos for Fareed Zakaria GPS." Jan 20, 2016, www.youtube.com/watch?v=hF2RLIxJ-8g. Accessed Nov 14, 2016.

Economics / Fiscal Policy

Are You Part of Justin Trudeau's Middle Class?

- Akin, David. "Are you in Justin Trudeau's middle class? Not if you're retired ." *Ottawa Sun*, Apr 03, 2014, www.ottawasun.com/2014/04/03/are-you-in-justin-trudeaus-middle-class-not-if-youre-retired. Accessed Nov 14, 2016.
- Statistics Canada, "Median total income, by family type, by province and territory ." *Statistics Canada*, Jun 14, 2016, www.statcan.gc.ca/tables-tableaux/sum-som/l01/cst01/famil108a-eng.htm. Accessed Nov 14, 2016.
- Kennedy, Mark. "Justin Trudeau on why he's the real alternative." *Ottawa Citizen*, Jun 18, 2015, ottawacitizen.com/news/politics/q-and-a-justin-trudeau-on-why-hes-the-real-alternative. Accessed Nov 14, 2016.

We Need the Middle Class To Feel More Confident

- Akin, David. "Are you in Justin Trudeau's middle class? Not if you're retired ." *Ottawa Sun*, Apr 03, 2014, www.ottawasun.com/2014/04/03/are-you-in-justin-trudeaus-middle-class-not-if-youre-retired. Accessed Nov 14, 2016.
- Statistics Canada, "Median total income, by family type, by province and territory ." *Statistics Canada*, Jun 14, 2016, www.statcan.gc.ca/tables-tableaux/sum-som/l01/cst01/famil108a-eng.htm. Accessed Nov 14, 2016.

- o Kennedy, Mark. "Justin Trudeau on why he's the real alternative." *Ottawa Citizen*, Jun 18, 2015, ottawacitizen.com/news/politics/q-and-a-justin-trudeau-on-why-hes-the-real-alternative. Accessed Nov 14, 2016.
- o Gaudet, Kevin. "Deficits, debt & disappointment." *The Taxpayer*, 2009, www.taxpayer.com/media/CoverStory24-27WEB.pdf. Accessed Nov 14, 2016.
- o Wikipedia. "Canadian public debt." *Wikipedia*, Dec 20, 2016, en.wikipedia.org/wiki/Canadian_public_debt. Accessed Nov 14, 2016.
- o Wikipedia. "List of Canadian federal parliaments." *Wikipedia*, Mar 17, 2016, en.wikipedia.org/wiki/Canadian_public_debt. Accessed Nov 14, 2016.
- o US Debt Clock, http://www.usdebtclock.org/index.html, Accessed Nov 14, 2016.

Promise Kept or Promise Broken?

- o CBC News, "Trudeau tracker: Has the prime minister kept his promise on home mail delivery?" *CBC News*, Apr 27, 2016, www.cbc.ca/news/politics/trudeau-tracker-home-delivery-canada-post-1.3554951. Accessed Nov 25, 2016.
- o CBC News, "Judy Foote 'not ruling out anything' in Canada Post review." *CBC News*, May 5, 2016, www.cbc.ca/news/politics/foote-canada-post-mail-delivery-1.3565888. Accessed Nov 25, 2016.
- o Press, Jordan and Pedwell, Terry. "Door-to-door mail delivery could return after Canada Post review." *CTV News*, May 5, 2016, www.ctvnews.ca/politics/door-to-door-mail-delivery-could-return-after-canada-post-review-1.2888724. Accessed Nov 25, 2016.
- o Government of Canada. "Canada Post in the digital age: Discussion paper." *Government of Canada*, September 2016, www.tpsgc-pwgsc.gc.ca/examendepostescanada-canadapostreview/rapport-report/consult-eng.html. Accessed Nov 25, 2016.

Small Businesses are Frauds and Tax Evaders

- o Justin Trudeau in an interview with CBC's Peter Mansbridge on *The National*, September 8, 2015

- Kenney, Jason. "Twitter Post." *Twitter.com*, Sep 9, 2015, twitter.com/jkenney/status/641687943099359232/photo/1?ref_sr c=twsrc%5Etfw. Accessed Nov 12, 2016.
- Press , Jordan. "Trudeau Says Wealthiest Canadians Using Small Business Tax Rate to Avoid Taxes." *Globe and Mail*, Sep 10, 2015, theglobeandmail.com/report-on-business/small-business/sb-money/trudeau-says-wealthiest-canadians-using-small-business-tax-rate-to-avoid-taxes/article26306519/. Accessed Nov 1, 2016.
- Canadian Federation of Independent Business, "A look at small business and the self-employed in Canada." *Canadian Federation of Independent Business*, 2015, www.cfib-fcei.ca/english/article/6071-sme-profiles.html. Accessed Nov 3, 2016.
- Innovation, Science and Economic Development Canada, "Key Small Business Statistics - June 2016." *Innovation, Science and Economic Development Canada*, June 6, 2016, www.ic.gc.ca/eic/site/061.nsf/eng/03022.html. Accessed Dec 2, 2016.

Government's Shouldn't Go Into Debt

- Trudeau, Justin. "Justin Trudeau CNN interview in Davos for Fareed Zakaria GPS." Jan 20, 2016, www.youtube.com/watch?v=hF2RLIxJ-8g. Accessed Nov 14, 2016.
- Cheadle, Bruce. "Federal Budget 2016: Liberals project $30B deficit and do not plan a return to surplus by 2019." National Post, Mar 22, 2016, news.nationalpost.com/news/canada/canadian-politics/federal-budget-2016-liberals-project-30b-deficit-with-no-plan-to-return-to-a-surplus-by-2019. Accessed Nov 5, 2016.

Deficits measure growth and government success

- Eugenio, Michael. "Trudeau becoming a walking, talking attack ad against himself." *The Prince Aurthur Herald*, Feb 18, 2014, princearthurherald.com/en/politics-2/trudeau-walking-attack-ad-345. Accessed Nov 2, 2016.
- Valiante, Giuseppe. "Harper calls Trudeau's stance on eliminating deficits 'magical'." *Toronto Sun*, Feb 12, 2014,

www.torontosun.com/2014/02/12/harper-calls-trudeaus-stance-on-eliminating-deficits-magical. Accessed Nov 15, 2016.

Growing the Economy from the Heart Outwards

o   The Canadian Press, "Trudeau says Liberals determined to grow economy 'from the heart outwards'." *Globe and Mail*, Aug. 12, 2015, www.theglobeandmail.com/news/politics/trudeau-says-liberals-determined-to-grow-economy-from-the-heart-outwards/article25940563/. Accessed Nov 22, 2016.

o   Shah, Maryam. "Trudeau determined to grow economy 'from the heart outwards'." *Toronto Sun*, Aug 12, 2015, www.torontosun.com/2015/08/12/trudeau-determined-to-grow-economy-from-the-heart-outwards. Accessed Nov 22, 2016.

o   CBC News, "Trudeau pledge to grow economy 'from the heart outwards' greeted with mockery." *CBC News*, Aug 13, 2015, www.cbc.ca/news/politics/trudeau-heart-economy-care-bears-1.3190219. Accessed Nov 22, 2016.

We Must Price Carbon!

o   Payton, Laura. "Justin Trudeau defends performance as 2013 draws to close." *CBC News*, Dec 11, 2013, www.cbc.ca/news/politics/justin-trudeau-defends-performance-as-2013-draws-to-close-1.2460445. Accessed Nov 16, 2016.

o   Gunter, Lorne. "Trudeau's carbon tax will hurt Canada's economy." *Edmonton Sun*, July 8, 2014, www.torontosun.com/2014/07/08/trudeaus-carbon-tax-will-hurt-canadas-economy. Accessed Nov 16, 2016.

o   Etam, Terry. "Saudi oil filling a New Brunswick refinery – what kind of a domestic energy policy is that?" *BOE Report*, Jan 25, 2016, boereport.com/2016/01/25/saudi-oil-filling-a-new-brunswick-refinery-what-kind-of-an-energy-policy-is-that/. Accessed Nov 16, 2016.

o   Cattaneo, Claudia. "As oilsands punished, tanker loads of cheap Saudi oil sail into Canadian ports daily." *Financial Post*, Feb 9, 2016, business.financialpost.com/news/energy/as-politicians-gloat-about-climate-leadership-saudi-arabias-oil-is-dumped-in-canada. Accessed Nov 16, 2016.

Social Issues / Human Rights

- Rebel Staff. "COVER UP: Parents, student CONFIRM refugee children choke, slap Canadian kids." *TheRebel.Media*, Apr 18, 2016, www.therebel.media/excerpt_halifax_refugee_bullying_cover_up , Accessed Dec 1, 2016.
- Hall, Chris. "Justin Trudeau's delay in resettling 25,000 Syrian refugees may be a smart political move." *CBC News*, Nov 25, 2015, www.cbc.ca/news/politics/justin-trudeau-syrian-refugees-canada-1.3335517. Accessed Dec 1, 2016.

Justin Trudeau is offended by the word "barbaric"

- Weese, Bryn, "Honour killings term angers Trudeau." *Toronto Sun*, www.torontosun.com/news/canada/2011/03/14/17610021.html. Accessed Nov 30, 2016.
- Toronto Star Staff Writer. "Trudeau ignites storm after 'barbaric' comments of honour killings." *Toronto Star*, Mar 15, 2011, www.thestar.com/news/canada/2011/03/15/trudeau_ignites_stor m_after_barbaric_comments_of_honour_killings.html, Accessed Nov 30, 2016.

"The Liberal Party of Canada does not discriminate"

- McParland, Kelly. "Kelly McParland: New holes in Justin Trudeau's abortion declaration." *National Post*, May 21, 2014, news.nationalpost.com/full-comment/kelly-mcparland-new-holes-in-justin-trudeaus-abortion-declaration. Accessed Nov 30, 2016.
- Urback, Robyn. "Robyn Urback: Why Justin Trudeau's abortion pledge is an insult to Canadian women." *National Post*, May 22, 2014, news.nationalpost.com/full-comment/robyn-urback-why-justin-trudeaus-abortion-pledge-is-an-insult-to-canadian-women. Accessed Nov 30, 2016.

"Faithful Catholic" attends Planned Parenthood fundraiser

- Craine, Patrick. "Tory MP blasts legal-abortion supporter Justin Trudeau over talk to Catholic students." *LifeSiteNews.com*, Nov

3, 2011, www.lifesitenews.com/news/tory-mp-blasts-pro-abort-trudeau-over-talk-to-catholic-students. Accessed Nov 26, 2016.

o Baklinski, Peter. "Justin Trudeau: sex-selective abortion a 'right'; Liberals won't consider ban." *LifeSiteNews.com*, May 23, 2014, www.lifesitenews.com/news/justin-trudeau-sex-selective-abortion-a-right-liberals-wont-consider-ban. Accessed Nov 26, 2016.

o Weatherbe, Steve. "Justin Trudeau attends Planned Parenthood fundraiser: assistant wins sex toy." *LifeSiteNews.com*, Oct 17, 2014, www.lifesitenews.com/news/justin-trudeau-attends-planned-parenthood-fundraiser-assistant-wins-sex-toy. Accessed Nov 26, 2016.

o Baklinski, Peter. "Excommunicate Catholic pro-abort Justin Trudeau, says outspoken newswoman." *LifeSiteNews.com*, Apr 16, 2014, www.lifesitenews.com/news/excommunicate-catholic-pro-abort-justin-trudeau-says-outspoken-newswoman. Accessed Nov 26, 2016.

o Baklinski, Peter. "'Prime act of pastoral charity' to deny pro-abortion politicians Communion: Cardinal Burke." *LifeSiteNews.com*, Mar 20, 2014, www.lifesitenews.com/news/prime-act-of-pastoral-charity-to-deny-pro-abortion-politicians-communion-ca. Accessed Nov 26, 2016.

o Westen, John-Henry. "How the newest Canadian bishop helped a 13-year-old say no to abortion." *LifeSiteNews.com*, May 13, 2014, www.lifesitenews.com/news/how-the-newest-canadian-bishop-helped-a-13-year-old-say-no-to-abortion. Accessed Nov 26, 2016.

o Craine, Patrick. "Cardinal Collins to Catholic Trudeau: Your abortion policy would ban Pope Francis from Liberal Party." *LifeSiteNews.com*, May 14, 2014, www.lifesitenews.com/news/torontos-cardinal-pens-letter-to-trudeau-notes-pope-francis-would-be-banned. Accessed Nov 26, 2016.

o Westen, John-Henry. "Ottawa archbishop on Trudeau: If you dissent on life issues, you're not a Catholic in good standing." *LifeSiteNews.com*, May 14, 2014, www.lifesitenews.com/news/ottawa-archbishop-on-trudeau-if-you-dissent-on-life-issues-youre-not-a-cath. Accessed Nov 26, 2016.

Justin Trudeau's Ethical Lobotomy on Abortion

o   DiManno, Rosie. "On abortion, Justin Trudeau imposes ethical lobotomy on Liberals." *Toronto Star*, May 16, 2014, www.thestar.com/news/gta/2014/05/16/on_abortion_justin_trude au_imposes_ethical_lobotomy_on_liberals.html. Accessed Nov 26, 2016.

o   Berthiaume, Lee. "Justin Trudeau faces scrutiny on abortion, prostitution, physician-assisted death." *Ottawa Citizen*, June 11, 2014, ottawacitizen.com/news/politics/justin-trudeau-faces-scrutiny-on-abortion-prostitution-physician-assisted-death. Accessed Nov 26, 2016.

o   Proussalidis, Daniel. "Tory MP slams Trudeau on sex-selective abortion." *Toronto Sun*, May 26, 2014, www.torontosun.com/2014/05/26/opponents-give-trudeau-kid-glove-treatment-on-sex-selective-abortion. Accessed Nov 26, 2016.

o   Batra, Adrienne. "Trudeau keeps it simple." *Toronto Sun*, May 24, 2014, www.torontosun.com/2014/05/23/trudeau-keeps-it-simple. Accessed Nov 26, 2016.

Justin Trudeau and Sex-Selective Abortion

o   Proussalidis, Daniel. "Tory MP slams Trudeau on sex-selective abortion." *Toronto Sun*, May 26, 2014, www.torontosun.com/2014/05/26/opponents-give-trudeau-kid-glove-treatment-on-sex-selective-abortion. Accessed Nov 26, 2016.

o   Baklinski, Peter. "Justin Trudeau: sex-selective abortion a 'right'; Liberals won't consider ban." *LifeSiteNews.com*, May 23, 2014, www.lifesitenews.com/news/justin-trudeau-sex-selective-abortion-a-right-liberals-wont-consider-ban. Accessed Nov 26, 2016.

Workplace Violence is Okay… if You Are Justin Trudeau

o   Maloney, Ryan. "Trudeau Apologizes To House Of Commons For 'Failing To Live Up To A Higher Standard'." *The Huffington Post Canada*, May 19, 2016, huffingtonpost.ca/2016/05/19/justin-trudeau-house-commons-apology-dustup_n_10046340.html. Accessed Nov 5, 2016.

o   Akin, David. "Elbowed by Trudeau and now under attack,

Brosseau asks: 'Do I have to justify how hard I was hit in the breast?'." *David Akin's On The Hill*, May 20th, 2016, blogs.canoe.com/davidakin/politics/after-trudeau-whacks-her-brosseau-asks-do-i-have-justify-how-hard-i-was-hit-in-the-breast/. Accessed Nov 5, 2016.

Justin Trudeau's Flip-Flop on Guns

o   Mas, Susana. "Trudeau calls long-gun registry 'a failure'." *CBC News*, Dec 1, 2012, www.cbc.ca/news/politics/trudeau-calls-long-gun-registry-a-failure-1.1278739. Accessed Nov 5, 2016.

o   The Canadian Press. "Trudeau calls long-gun registry 'a failure'." *CBC News*, Dec 3, 2012, www.cbc.ca/news/politics/justin-trudeau-explains-his-gun-policy-as-debate-flares-1.1224400. Accessed Nov 5, 2016.

o   Hervieux-Payette, Senator Céline. "Bill S-231 An Act to amend the Firearms Act, the Criminal Code and the Defence Production Act." *Parliament of Canada*, Jun 11, 2015, parl.gc.ca/HousePublications/Publication.aspx?Language=E&Mode=1&DocId=8043166&File=4&Col=1. Accessed Nov 5, 2016.

o   Hervieux-Payette, Senator Céline. "Strengthening Canadians' Security and Promoting Hunting and Recreational Shooting." *The Honourable Céline Hervieux-Payette Blog*, Jun 11, 2015, eurekablog.ca/en/articles/politics/national/strenghtening-canadians-security-and-promoting-hunting-and-recreational-shooting/. Accessed Nov 5, 2016.

Repeal Mandatory Minimum Sentences for Pedophiles

o   Lilley, Brian. "Scandals fade, policy matters." *Ottawa Sun*, Nov 21, 2013, ottawasun.com/2013/11/21/scandals-fade-policy-matters. Accessed Nov 5, 2016.

o   Ibbitson, John. "Tories on e-snooping: 'Stand with us or with the child pornographers'." *Globe and Mail*, Feb. 13, 2012, theglobeandmail.com/news/politics/tories-on-e-snooping-stand-with-us-or-with-the-child-pornographers/article545799/. Accessed Nov 5, 2016.

o   Gunter, Lorne. "Mandatory sentences make sense." *Edmonton Sun*, Nov 19, 2013, edmontonsun.com/2013/11/19/mandatory-sentences-make-sense. Accessed Nov 5, 2016.

o   Court Of Appeal For British Columbia, "R. v. Nghiem, 2009 BCCA 170." *Canadian Legal Information Institute*, April 9,

2009,
canlii.org/en/bc/bcca/doc/2009/2009bcca170/2009bcca170.html.
Accessed Nov 5, 2016.

Security, Foreign Affairs / Terrorism

The Temporary Foreign Worker Program

o   Trudeau, Justin. "Justin Trudeau: How to fix the broken
    temporary foreign worker program." *Globe and Mail*, May 5,
    2014,
    thestar.com/opinion/commentary/2014/05/05/how_to_fix_the_br
    oken_temporary_foreign_worker_program_justin_trudeau.html.
    Accessed Nov 9, 2016.
o   Ivison, John. "Trudeau hired nanny under temporary foreign
    worker program — before he became a vocal critic of it."
    National Post, May 27, 2016,
    news.nationalpost.com/news/canada/canadian-politics/trudeau-
    hired-nanny-under-temporary-foreign-worker-program-before-
    he-became-vocal-critic-of-the-program. Accessed Nov 9, 2016.
o   Taylor, Stephen. "Justin Trudeau asks for Temporary Foreign
    Worker permits." *StephenTaylor.ca*, May 2013,
    stephentaylor.ca/2013/04/justin-trudeau-asks-for-temporary-
    foreign-worker-permits/. Accessed Nov 9, 2016.
o   Chase, Steven. "Tories release letter by Trudeau asking for
    temporary foreign workers for his riding." *Globe and Mail*, Apr
    17, 2013, theglobeandmail.com/news/politics/tories-release-
    letter-by-trudeau-asking-for-temporary-foreign-workers-for-his-
    riding/article11339272/. Accessed Nov 9, 2016.

We will repeal the parts that are problematic with C-51

o   Kennedy, Mark. "Q and A: Justin Trudeau on why he's the real
    alternative." *Ottawa Citizen*, Jun 18, 2015,
    ottawacitizen.com/news/politics/q-and-a-justin-trudeau-on-why-
    hes-the-real-alternative. Accessed Nov 15, 2016.
o   Mazigh, Monia. "Liberals Need The Political Courage To Finally
    Repeal Bill C-51." *Huffington Post*, Jul 13, 2016,
    huffingtonpost.ca/monia-mazigh/repeal-bill-c-
    51_b_10952876.html. Accessed Nov 15, 2016.

o Bozinoff, Ph.D., Lorne.. "Support for Bill C51 waning." *Forum Research*, Apr 9, 2015, poll.forumresearch.com/post/256/most-see-bill-having-negative-effect-on-their-lives/. Accessed Nov 15, 2016.

o Watters, Haydn. "C-51, controversial anti-terrorism bill, is now law. So, what changes?" *CBC News*, Jun 18, 2015, cbc.ca/news/politics/c-51-controversial-anti-terrorism-bill-is-now-law-so-what-changes-1.3108608. Accessed Nov 5, 2016.

o Government of Canada, "Security of Canada Information Sharing Act." *Government of Canada*, Aug 1, 2015, laws-lois.justice.gc.ca/eng/acts/S-6.9/. Accessed Nov 5, 2016.

o Mitrovica, Andrew. "Why nobody should bet on Trudeau 'fixing' C-51." *iPolitics.ca*, Dec 9th, 2015, ipolitics.ca/2015/12/09/why-nobody-should-bet-on-trudeau-fixing-c-51/. Accessed Nov 5, 2016.

o Hall, Chris. "Trudeau tracker: Promised changes to anti-terrorism law C-51 still months away." *CBC News*, May 17, 2016, www.cbc.ca/news/politics/trudeau-tracker-anti-terrorism-bill-1.3586337. Accessed Nov 5, 2016.

o Canadian Journalists for Free Expression. "The Fight to Kill C-51 Isn't Over." *Canadian Journalists for Free Expression*, Jul 21, 2016, www.cjfe.org/bill_c_51_is_still_law_here_s_how_we_can_repeal_it. Accessed Nov 5, 2016.

Justin Trudeau's Visits "Stone Them to Death" Imam

o Valiante, Giuseppe. "Tories criticize Trudeau for visiting mosque whose imam supports stoning." *Toronto Sun*, Oct 8, 2014, torontosun.com/2014/10/08/tories-criticize-trudeau-for-visiting-mosque-whose-imam-supports-stoning. Accessed Nov 5, 2016.

o Rath, Ted. "Controversial imam whose mosque hosted Canada Day citizenship ceremony denies he supported stoning women or cutting hands of thieves." *Toronto Sun*, Jul 4, 2016, torontosun.com/2016/07/04/controversial-imam-whose-mosque-hosted-canada-day-citizenship-ceremony-denies-he-supported-stoning-women-or-cutting-hands-of-thieves. Accessed Nov 5, 2016.

o Ontario Superior Court of Justice, "R. v. Ahmed, 2014 ONSC 5367." *Canadian Legal Information Institute*, Sept 18, 2014, canlii.org/en/on/onsc/doc/2014/2014onsc5367/2014onsc5367.html. Accessed Nov 5, 2016.

o Ontario Superior Court of Justice, "R. v. Ahmed, 2014 ONSC

6153." *Canadian Legal Information Institute*, Oct 23, 2014, canlii.org/en/on/onsc/doc/2014/2014onsc6153/2014onsc6153.ht ml. Accessed Nov 5, 2016.

Trudeau and the Reviving Islamic Spirit Convention

○ Assadollahi, Shabnam. "Trudeau's Multiculturalism!" *Dr. Rich Swier Blog*, Aug 21, 2016, drrichswier.com/2016/08/21/trudeaus-multiculturalism/. Accessed Nov 5, 2016.
-Halevi, Jonathan. "Trudeau: Reviving the Islamic Spirit convention exemplifies 'our shared beliefs'." *CIJ News*, Dec 29, 2015, en.cijnews.com/?p=17895. Accessed Nov 5, 2016.
○ Hume, Jessica. "Trudeau under fire for attending controversial Islamic group's event." *Toronto Sun*, Jul 16, 2013, torontosun.com/2013/07/16/trudeau-under-fire-for-attending-controversial-islamic-groups-event. Accessed Nov 5, 2016.

Trudeau's Terrorist Apologetics

○ Postmedia Network and The Canadian Press. "Liberals' answer to terrorists: Talk them through their feelings." *Toronto Sun*, Aug 17, 2016, torontosun.com/2016/08/17/trudeaus-answer-to-terrorists-talk-them-through-their-feelings. Accessed Nov 5, 2016.
○ Berthiaume, Lee. "Don't 'sit around trying to rationalize it': Harper slams Trudeau for response to Boston bombing." *National Post*, Apr 17, 2013, news.nationalpost.com/news/canada/canadian-politics/trudeaus-response-to-boston-marathon-bombing-was-unacceptable-made-excuses-for-terrorists-harper-says. Accessed Nov 5, 2016.
○ The Canadian Press. "Liberals to announce details of anti-terror program aimed at curbing radicalization." *Toronto Star*, Aug 14, 2016, thestar.com/news/canada/2016/08/14/liberals-to-announce-anti-terror-program-aimed-at-curbing-radicalization.html. Accessed Nov 5, 2016.
○ Wells, Paul. "No surprises in Trudeau's stance on terrorism: Paul Wells." *Toronto Star*, Aug 14, 2016, thestar.com/news/canada/2016/08/17/no-surprises-in-trudeaus-stance-on-terrorism-paul-wells.html. Accessed Nov 5, 2016.
○ Geddes, John. "Trudeau, Harper and the Boston bombings: Let's go back to the tape." *Maclean's*, Apr 18, 2013, macleans.ca/politics/ottawa/listening-closely-to-trudeau-on-

terrorism-and-harper-on-trudeaus-reaction/. Accessed Nov 5, 2016.

Convicted Terrorists Keep Your Passports

o Maloney, Ryan. "Bill C-24: Trudeau Says Terrorists Shouldn't Be Stripped Of Citizenship In Leaked Audio." *The Huffington Post Canada*, Sep 28, 2015, huffingtonpost.ca/2015/09/28/bill-c-24-trudeau-audio-conservatives_n_8206798.html. Accessed Nov 18, 2016.

o CTVNews.ca Staff. "In audio recording, Trudeau says Bill C-24 makes citizenship conditional upon 'good behaviour'." *CTV News*, Sep 27, 2015, ctvnews.ca/politics/in-audio-recording-trudeau-says-bill-c-24-makes-citizenship-conditional-upon-good-behaviour-1.2583849. Accessed Nov 18, 2016.

Is Brad Wall promoting hatred against Muslims?

o Liberal Party of Canada (Ontario). "Condemning All Forms of Islamophobia." *Liberal Party of Canada*, May 28, 2016, winnipeg2016.liberal.ca/policy/condemning-all-forms-of-islamophobia/. Accessed Nov 18, 2016.

o Wall, Premier Brad. "Letter to Prime Minister Justin Trudeau." *Premier Brad Wall*, Nov 16, 2015, drive.google.com/file/d/0BzOQiYxD44uwWDJkRms5TzFMOU 0/view. Accessed Nov 18, 2016.

o Friscolanti, Michael. "Should the Trudeau Liberals rethink their plan for Syrian refugees?" *Maclean's*, Nov 16, 2015, macleans.ca/politics/ottawa/should-the-trudeau-liberals-rethink-their-plan-for-syrian-refugees/. Accessed Nov 18, 2016.

o National Council of Canadian Muslims. "Charter for Inclusive Communities." *National Council of Canadian Muslims*, Jun 29, 2016, www.nccm.ca/charter/. Accessed Nov 18, 2016.

o Fatah, Tarek. "Canada home to Islamic radicals." *Toronto Sun*, May 24, 2016, torontosun.com/2016/05/24/canada-home-to-islamic-radicals. Accessed Nov 18, 2016.

o Canadian Human Rights Commission. "What is discrimination?" *Canadian Human Rights Commission*, May 24, 2016, chrc-ccdp.ca/eng/content/what-discrimination. Accessed Nov 9, 2016.

o Government of Canada. "What is discrimination?" *Criminal Code of Canada Section 319*, Apr 29, 2004, laws-lois.justice.gc.ca/eng/acts/C-46/section-319-20040429.html#wbcont. Accessed Nov 9, 2016.

Let's Whip out our CF-18s

- Janus, Andrea. "PMO decries Trudeau joke that Canada should not 'whip out our CF-18s'." *CTV News*, Oct 2, 2014, ctvnews.ca/politics/pmo-decries-trudeau-joke-that-canada-should-not-whip-out-our-cf-18s-1.2035759. Accessed Nov 9, 2016.
- Bryden, Joan. "Trudeau On Iraq: Harper Can't Just 'Whip Out Our CF-18s'." *Huffington Post*, Oct 2, 2014, huffingtonpost.ca/2014/10/02/justin-trudeau-iraq-combat-mission_n_5920670.html. Accessed Nov 9, 2016.
- CBC News. "Justin Trudeau - Whip out our CF-18s and show them how big they are." *CBC News Video*, Oct 2, 2014, youtube.com/watch?v=ilXxSr_-vJ8. Accessed Nov 9, 2016.

I Admire China's Basic Dictatorship

- Baklinski, Peter. "Trudeau's 'admiration' of China's brutal 'dictatorship' learned on the knees of his father." LifeSiteNews.com, Nov 15, 2013, lifesitenews.com/opinion/trudeaus-admiration-of-chinas-brutal-dictatorship-learned-on-the-knees-of-h. Accessed Nov 9, 2016.
- CBC News. "Justin Trudeau's 'foolish' China remarks spark anger." CBC News, Nov 9, 2013, cbc.ca/news/canada/toronto/justin-trudeau-s-foolish-china-remarks-spark-anger-1.2421351. Accessed Nov 9, 2016.
- Wente, Margaret. "Justin Trudeau does ladies' night." Globe and Mail, Nov 12, 2013, theglobeandmail.com/opinion/justin-does-ladies-night/article15379289/. Accessed Nov 9, 2016.

Justin Trudeau on Fidel Castro - an International Laughing Stock

- Trudeau, Justin. "Statement by the Prime Minister of Canada on the death of former Cuban President Fidel Castro." Prime Minister of Canada, Nov 26, 2016, pm.gc.ca/eng/news/2016/11/26/statement-prime-minister-canada-death-former-cuban-president-fidel-castro. Accessed Nov 27, 2016.
- Den Tandt, Michael. "Earth to Trudeau — Fidel Castro was a brutal dictator, not a benevolent, grizzled uncle." National Post,

Nov 27, 2016, news.nationalpost.com/full-comment/michael-den-tandt-earth-to-trudeau. Accessed Nov 27, 2016.

o   Various Authors. "#trudeaueulogies." Twitter.com, Nov 27, 2016, twitter.com/hashtag/trudeaueulogies?src=hash. Accessed Nov 27, 2016.

o   Trudeau, Justin. "Rare Video. Justin Trudeau receive's Boo's at 2016 Grey Cup!" YouTube.com, Nov 28, 2016, youtube.com/watch?v=mgktEINkZcs. Accessed Nov 28, 2016.

o   Rainbow PUSH Coalition. "People The World Over Celebrate Fidel Castro" Facebook.com, Nov 26, 2016, facebook.com/Rainbow.PUSH/photos/a.314156062005612.7701 1.306935452727673/1181486655272544/?type=3&theater. Accessed Nov 28, 2016.

o   Amnesty International. "Fidel Castro's human rights legacy: A tale of two worlds." Amnesty International, Nov 26, 2016, amnesty.org/en/latest/news/2016/11/fidel-castro-s-human-rights-legacy-a-tale-of-two-worlds/. Accessed Nov 28, 2016.

Your support in the form of an honest review on both Amazon and Goodreads helps this book find more readers.

http://ChristopherDiArmani.net/Review-Trudeau-Book-on-Amazon

http://ChristopherDiArmani.net/Review-Trudeau-Book-on-Goodreads